"I love Colin McCartney. We've been friends for over a decade. I've read all his books. And this one is special. He deconstructs the things that need deconstruction, but he helps you reconstruct a better, more robust faith. He doesn't come with a wrecking ball, but rather has the precision of a surgeon. As Colin reminds us, the word *gospel* means 'good news' . . . but much of what you hear in the church doesn't sound like good news at all. Colin helps you cut through the funk of Christendom and get to the real good news of Jesus. That good news is that God is love, nothing more and nothing less. And anyone who tries to tell you otherwise is lying."

—**SHANE CLAIBORNE**, author, activist, and cofounder of Red Letter Christians

"In this engaging, insightful, and immensely practical work, Colin McCartney helps readers deconstruct their fear-based conceptions of God as well as their 'flat' ways of reading Scripture in order to help them reconstruct their conception of God in light of the revelation of God in Christ. I believe that readers who take this easy-to-read book to heart and who put into practice its wise instruction will discover a relationship with God and a way of reading Scripture that is as beautiful as it is transforming. I couldn't recommend a book more strongly than I recommend *Let the Light In*."

—**GREG BOYD**, theologian, author, and senior pastor of Woodland Hills Church

"Through sharing personal experiences, relying heavily on Scripture, and looking closely at church history, Colin McCartney contributes to the process of deconstruction, or in his own words, 'renovation,' regardless of whether you identify as a follower of Jesus or are skeptical. Above all, Colin draws us back to celebrate a 'lost treasure' that has been 'found,' which is that in Jesus Christ the fullness of God dwells. This revelation of a Jesus-like God brings healing to the distorted images of God that religion and bad theology have given us. As someone who is from, and also serves in, the inner city, I can see how this book will make sense of a lot of questions that have held us in bondage. Through seeing the love of God displayed in Jesus, I can also see the liberation from that bondage."

—**JORDAN THOMS**, rap artist and pastor of Warden Underground Community Church

"This is a must-read for those who are ready to be honest and transparent with their theological struggles. Through Colin McCartney's own spiritual journey, the reader is invited to join in deep personal reflection. Disturbing questions are validated and nagging doubts are acknowledged. The potential reward for participating in this exercise of deep reflection is worth the discomfort it may cause. It is honesty that will bring relief and allow truth to set you free."

—**WILLARD METZGER**, executive director of Citizens for Public Justice and former executive director of Mennonite Church Canada

"Colin McCartney has an uncanny ability to simplify complex theology in his explanation of who Jesus was and is. As he shares his own stories, we are invited to see how he deconstructs his childhood understanding of God to better follow Jesus daily in his ministry amid urban poverty. *Let the Light In* is a challenging, encouraging, and must-read book."

—**BRIAN BAUMAN**, retired mission minister for Mennonite Church Eastern Canada

"Whether you are a pastor, church member, or casual participant or are among the growing cadre of 'nones and dones,' Colin McCartney's book is a courageous challenge to all of us to reclaim Jesus as the center of who we are and all we are called to be. Getting to know Colin in the course of the journey unpacked in this book has been a blessing. Seeing Colin's journey influence a new generation of church planters has been and continues to be an inspiration! *Let the Light In* is a must-read for all our church planters."

—**NORM DYCK**, founder and team leader of INNOVATE Be the Change and mission minister for Mennonite Church Eastern Canada

"This important book deals with some of the key questions that many are afraid to ask and many leaders are afraid to tackle. Drawing on a broad range of teachers from the earliest centuries up to the present, and integrating his personal faith journey, Colin McCartney deals with simplistic ideas of a harsh, judgmental God, dictation theories of inspiration, the importance of Jesus as the living Word of God, and other questions that are causing many to leave more conservative churches. While it is highly unlikely that anyone will agree with every idea advanced, the issues raised deserve the attention of all thinking Christians. An easy-to-read and thought-provoking book."

—**MALCOM SEATH**, retired pharmaceutical executive and board member of numerous professional, business, and mission groups

LET THE
LIGHT IN

LET THE LIGHT IN

HEALING FROM DISTORTED IMAGES OF GOD

Colin McCartney

HERALD
PRESS

Harrisonburg, Virginia

Herald Press
PO Box 866, Harrisonburg, Virginia 22803
www.HeraldPress.com

Study guides are available for many Herald Press titles at
www.HeraldPress.com.

LET THE LIGHT IN
© 2021 by Herald Press, Harrisonburg, Virginia 22803. 800-245-7894.
  All rights reserved.
Library of Congress Control Number: 2021933210
International Standard Book Number: 978-1-5138-0809-3 (paperback);
  978-1-5138-0810-9 (hardcover); 978-1-5138-0811-6 (ebook)
Printed in United States of America
Cover and interior design by Merrill Miller

25 24 23 22 21   10 9 8 7 6 5 4 3 2 1

To all those who struggle with knowing that God loves them deeply. May you have power to grasp how wide and long and high and deep is the love of Christ, and to know this love that surpasses knowledge—that you may be filled to the measure of all the fullness of God.

CONTENTS

Foreword

SIGMUND FREUD POSITED that a person's concept of God was a projection of their own superego—their sense of morality shaped by what they have been taught. This poses a particular problem for the many evangelical Christians who have been indoctrinated with a concept of God derived largely from Jonathan Edwards' famous sermon "Sinners in the Hands of an Angry God." In this book, Colin McCartney calls us to instead conceive of God as being like Jesus, who in the fourteenth chapter of the gospel of John, said, "When you have seen me, you have seen the Father."

According to McCartney, the negative image of an angry and vindictive God is, in no small way, driving many thoughtful people from the church, even from Christianity itself. This book allows us to accompany McCartney on a journey of faith—influenced theologically by his ministry with the Mennonites—that led him to a new and deeper understanding of God as revealed in Jesus. He takes the reader from the God defined by the penal substitutionary doctrine of the atonement, who comes across as angry and vindictive, to the God defined by the *Christus Victor* doctrine of the atonement, who in the death and resurrection of Jesus, defeated all the dark forces of the universe. This Anabaptist thinking about God offers freedom from the fears and anxieties often generated by "fire and brimstone" preachers and will help the reader understand God as compassionate and forgiving, rather than as hyper-condemning and vengeful. I believe that upon finishing the book, the reader will likely say, "Oh, what a relief that is!"

McCartney wants us to understand more fully the God who came to earth in Jesus not to condemn the world, but to save it. He is especially hopeful that this book will teach us to read the Bible through "the lens of Jesus." When we do this, he suggests, we will find a God who, even in the midst of tough Old Testament stories, is working to overcome pain and suffering while defeating the works of the devil. The author is no stranger to tough stories himself. Readers will appreciate the illustrations from McCartney's own life, many from his years of ministry among "at risk" young people in derelict government housing in Toronto, Canada, and in Camden, New Jersey.

McCartney does not "water down" Jesus by making him a God we can walk all over without dire consequence, nor does he present the God conjured up by the young man who once said to me, "Jesus likes to forgive, and I like to sin, so it's a perfect arrangement." McCartney does not give us a God who offers "cheap grace." The God he presents takes our sin very seriously, but in his love will not let us go, no matter what.

Anticipating those who may accuse him of relativism, McCartney contends that any reading of early Christian writers will show that he is in step with the church fathers (be sure to read his endnotes). In fact, the writings of the early church will prove attractive to many who have left the church of today. Jesus said, "I, if I may be lifted up from the earth, will draw all men unto myself" (John 12:32 YLT). That is the image of God revealed in Jesus, and that is the image of God that McCartney wants us to hold up for the church in today's world. He makes a solid case when he says that many who have left the church have completely failed to grasp what God is all about. The God they rejected was a faulty image of God.

This book does not set out to answer all the tough questions we may have about God, but Colin McCartney does guide us into new ways of thinking that in turn may help us answer some of those questions for ourselves. *Let the Light In* presents sophisticated biblical research and theological reflection in readable fashion for the Christian layperson. I believe that anyone who carefully reads this book will welcome its wisdom and Christ-focused insight. I certainly do.

—*Tony Campolo*
Speaker, author, sociologist, pastor, social activist, and passionate follower of Jesus

Introduction

A Must-Read before You Jump Right In

AS A CHILD OF IMMIGRANTS, I often wonder at the great courage it must have taken for my father to leave his family and friends to move from Ireland to Canada all on his own. I can only imagine how he felt when he first stepped onto that ship in the Port of Belfast. His heart must have been beating double time, coursing with adrenaline and fear at leaving all that was known and comfortable to him. Here he was, alone and frightened, with nothing but a small suitcase as his only possession, on a ship set sail to cross the Atlantic Ocean. I am sure he must have fought back tears over leaving friends and family as he waved goodbye to the life he knew and the country he loved.

This experience raises the question: Why would anyone immigrate? What possesses a person to walk away from everything they know and everyone they love to enter an unknown land?

There can only be two explanations for such a decision. There is either a great love waiting for them on another shore, or there is a hopeful promise of a better life beckoning them to move on. I have seen the power of these motivations in the lives of friends who have left Canada to be with someone they love who lives in a foreign country. That's an act of great love. Other people I know have left their country for the promise of a better life in a new land. That is an act of great hope.

In some ways, my father and I have a lot in common. Although I don't feel the need to leave my physical country, I have felt compelled to leave my country of spiritual origin for the hopeful promise of a better life and a deeper relationship with the One I love. Enflamed by the love of God, I have been emboldened to leave the safe religious shores to which I am accustomed, and to sail through rough waters to join God in a new land. I haven't gone a long way off from where I began, but I definitely have moved on from where I once was. This process has been difficult for me. It has been hard to wave goodbye to familiar doctrines and the religious life I knew since childhood. But God keeps calling me from the familiar to the unfamiliar, and from the safety of my comfortable spiritual constructs to a more wild and adventurous faith that allows me to be closer by his side.

Many people use the term *deconstruction* to describe the journey of reshaping their faith. For me, this process of deconstruction has been more like a much-needed renovation of my soul, spurred onward by a holy uneasiness from within. As I go through this process, I find great comfort in knowing that the divine architect values my life so much that he never settles for an unfinished product. God has far bigger and better plans for me, and his Son is always at work to fulfill the finished work of Christ in me.[1] The carpenter from Nazareth goes to work tearing down aspects of my belief system that have become obstacles to my growth, making room in my soul to encounter more of the fullness of God. This renovating process can be painful, as Jesus breaks down the false security of my religiosity by putting a sledgehammer to doctrines that I once held dear. All the wood, hay, and straw that my interior life had been built on is ripped out to make room for the gold that Jesus wants to rebuild inside me.[2]

The great sixteenth-century Carmelite mystic Saint John of the Cross had a different take on this deconstruction process.[3] He called it "the dark night of the soul," a journey that each of us has to go through to grow closer to God.[4] Saint John taught that during "the dark night of the soul," we are stripped of all the worldly and spiritual things we once held dear. The reason for this purging is because these things can often become an end to themselves, idols that can get in the way of truly loving God. For some of us, this purging might mean that the spiritual acts of worship that once nourished our souls no longer have a positive effect on us. After all, even good things can become false gods if we let them! Regular church attendance, reading Scripture, worship through music, times of prayer, certainty of doctrinal beliefs, and the like can take the place of God in our lives, filling us with a false spirituality known as religion. By religion, I mean a system we can easily fall into that prioritizes rules and religious ritual over Jesus as the center of our lives. So God, in his loving mercy, begins to chip away at our entanglement with these acts of religion by causing them to lose the power they once held over us. What used to feed our souls no longer does, and we feel spiritually dry, or in some cases, we might even feel that God has abandoned us. However, this is not the case.

God hasn't left us at all. Instead, God is realigning our spiritual priorities. The carpenter from Nazareth is at work in our lives.

I can relate to what Saint John is teaching us, as I often experience how easy it is for my soul to wander away from Jesus. I'll never forget the day I was speaking at a large conference when I ran into Bruce Wilkinson, the author of the New York Times bestseller *The Prayer of Jabez*.

As we waited in the speakers' room, we had a wonderful conversation concerning our personal faith struggles. One thing Bruce shared with me was that we start out our faith walk with our priorities in order. When we first come to Christ, we give him the throne of our lives. However, as time goes on, we tend to allow other things to crowd Jesus off the throne of our lives. Jesus is slowly pushed aside by day-to-day activities, religious formalities, and even acts of service. It is important to realize that it is often the little things that get in the way, not the obvious sins. Jesus is no longer on the throne. Then Bruce said something profound to me. "Always remember. Jesus has his way of taking back the throne."

Welcome to the world of deconstruction.

My deconstruction started when my world was turned upside down by three sudden tragedies that took place in a nine-month span in my life—the murder of one of our young staff, followed by the drowning of a child I knew, and then an accident in which I broke my neck on a beach in Maui. None of these catastrophes were from the hands of God, for God does not delight in calamities. This one thing I do know is that life tends to stir up all sorts of challenges on its own yet through it all, God's comforting presence is with us in our times of trouble.

During my time of suffering, many things I was taught and believed about God and the Bible no longer made any sense.[5] I was lost in a swirl of confusion as my spiritual, emotional, and physical foundations were torn apart in a tsunami of grief, pain, and doubts. My safe religious life of answers and order was now demolished, and I had two choices to make. I could chuck the whole thing in one big act of avoidance. Or I could embrace the tragedy I was experiencing and learn from it. I chose the latter and allowed my tragic circumstances to instruct me. As painful as my choice was, it was there, in all my brokenness, that I discovered God, the real God! Not the god that was just a religious term for someone I had to believe in as part of a theological creed. No, it was here, in my deepest trials, that I experienced the true living God who has always been with me all along!

I'll never forget an experience I had one day while recuperating in the hospital from my broken neck. I had what I can only explain as a vision from God. This scared me, as I had been taught that these types of experiences were far too dangerous, as they upset the apple cart of order that my religious beliefs so deeply cherished. Yet now, in my time of suffering, I was having a mystical encounter with God. It came in the form of a dream in which I found myself in a garden with Jesus, who was pointing at weeds that, with my approval, he would remove and replace with the most beautiful flowers I had ever seen. This went on for a while as my garden slowly emptied of the many weeds that had infested its soil, until all that was left was a glorious abundance of beautiful flowers! The next day I awoke but quickly forgot about my dream. However, a few weeks later I was reminded of my dream in a supernatural manner when I read the following quote about prayer from the great mystic Saint Teresa of Ávila.

> Beginners must realize that in order to give delight to the Lord they are starting to cultivate a garden on very barren

soil, full of abominable weeds. His Majesty pulls up the weeds and plants good seed. Now let us keep in mind that all of this is already done by the time a soul is determined to practice prayer and has begun to make use of it. And with the help of God we must strive like good gardeners to get these plants to grow and take pains to water them so that they don't wither but come to bud and flower and give forth a most pleasant fragrance to provide refreshment for this Lord of ours. Then He will often come to take delight in this garden and find His joy among these virtues.[6]

I had no recollection of ever having read Saint Teresa's description of the soul as a garden, thanks to my religious upbringing's frowning upon mystics like her. Yet her words described what I had seen during my dream. This was the beginning of many deep encounters I had with God that went beyond anything I was taught to believe. I was now on the journey of the deconstruction of my soul, and my religious background fought against it each step of the way. When I had the dream of my soul as a garden, I experienced how safe it is to be in the presence of a loving God. I saw how the weeds were my sins. They are ugly, useless, and hurtful to others and myself. My old religion made me feel guilty of these things and created such a high degree of shame that it kept me away from God. But now, having been stripped bare of my false religious teachings, I found myself in God's presence. In this sacred space of vulnerability, I didn't feel any shame about allowing Jesus to see me as I truly am. Nor did I ever feel that Christ was accusing me because of the weeds in my soul. Jesus actually smiled at me as I showed him my weeds. He knew that by exposing my weeds he could now replace them with his flowers. The Spirit was doing great soul work in the chaos and disorder of my life as I honestly and safely dealt with my personal sins, doubts, fears, and failures in front of a loving God. But for this to happen, I had to be willing to leave the guilt-inducing shores of my current faith system to get to where God wanted me to be. When faced with my questions and doubts, I had to trust God's love to safely embrace deconstruction instead of fleeing deeper into the shadows of a shallow religion.

* * * *

When we go through experiences of deconstruction, some people might falsely accuse us of being unfaithful to God because of the questions we are asking about our faith. Doubts about what we believe begin to pop up in our minds that can shake us to our core. When this happens, our community of faith, both friends and family, can begin to feel very uncomfortable about our journey. This is especially the case for those who are caught up in religion.

Saint John of the Cross shares much-needed wisdom concerning this reaction to faith deconstruction.

> It will happen to individuals that while they are being conducted by God along a sublime path of dark contemplation and aridity, in which they feel lost, they will meet someone in the midst of the fullness of their darknesses, trials, conflicts, and temptations who, in the style of Job's comforters (Job 4:8-11), will proclaim that all this is due to melancholia, depression, or temperament, or to some hidden wickedness, and that as a result God has forsaken them. Therefore, the usual verdict is that these individuals must have lived an evil life since such trials afflict them. Others will tell them that they are falling back since they find no satisfaction or

consolation as they previously did in the things of God. Such talk only doubles the trial of the poor soul.[7]

This wise saint gives us a clear description of what many people experience as they go through faith deconstruction—dryness, fullness of darkness, trials, lostness, and conflicts. However, Saint John of the Cross also holds out great hope for what is taking place, and reminds us that individuals who go through this *"are being conducted by God along a sublime path of dark contemplation and aridity."*[8]

The struggles, doubts, and fears that you may be experiencing are actually a wonderful act of God in your life. God is stripping away your dependence on religion, spiritual leaders, and pious rituals so your soul can be free of these false attachments and cry out desperately for God, and God alone, to fill you with his presence. God is at work. Deconstruction is a major way God destroys our old religious wineskins to replace them with new ones that can allow his life-giving wine to flow freely in our souls.[9]

So if you are feeling spiritually dry or are wrestling with beliefs you once held dear and that no longer make any sense to you, take heart. God may be at work reshaping you to experience him on a deeper level. Likewise, if you know people who are working out their faith by asking tough questions, be patient with them and do not judge them. Respect the spiritual process and growth they are going through. This is all a legitimate and even expected part of the spiritual life. In fact, it is a good and proper path of spiritual growth, as we are told by the author of Philippians: "Continue to work out your salvation with fear and trembling, for it is God who works in you to will and to act in order to fulfill his good purpose" (Philippians 2:12-13).

God is at work, and your soul is a precious construction site. Could this be what deconstruction means?

As you read this book, it is important that you understand that it is written in the belief that the Bible truly is from God. This high view of Scripture is the driving force behind my choice to address the theological "hot buttons" in this book, since they are often mistakenly used to support toxic views of God. You will find lots of scriptural references throughout this book. When I share the possibility that Jesus' death was not intended to appease an angry God, or that there is another way to understand Scripture, I do so in the spirit of the Bereans who were hungry for God's Word and examined everything they were taught through the Scriptures.[10] I encourage you to learn from the Bereans' practice of examining the Scriptures for God's truth by having an open Bible with you as you read this book.

I would never claim that what you are about to read reflects the musings of my own mind. My thoughts cannot compare to those of the great theologians from whom I learn, nor am I bold or foolish enough to claim that I have found a special revelation upon which to base the contents of this book. I take great comfort in knowing that everything you read on these pages has been around for many years. Wiser people than me, including some of the greatest minds in church history as well as Jesus, spoke in different ways of the great news that God is love. Understanding the magnificent reality that we live in the kingdom reign of God, and that this God who reigns does so with an unstoppable, relentless love, will change everything.[11] It will actually shape your brain and develop your emotional quotient so you are able to have a healthy self-image and see others in a positive light, as beloved children of our loving Father God.

Knowing God is love will also change how you read your Bible. When you read the Scriptures in light of the enemy-loving, radically forgiving, self-sacrificing God of unrelenting love proclaimed on the cross, you will be able to make sense of violent depictions attributed to God in the Old Testament as somewhat distorted depictions of God's true nature, as revealed in Jesus. Knowing that God is like Jesus will also transform the way you view certain doctrines such as the atonement (the reason behind the crucifixion), God's sovereignty, the holiness of God, and the meaning of God's wrath, as well as eschatology (the theology of end times).

Some of you will feel overwhelmed by what you are about to read. This book might challenge long-held beliefs or seem to contradict what you have been taught or what your church believes. If this is your experience, hang in there. Unfortunately, Western Christianity tends to punish people for asking questions about faith instead of recognizing that questions are part of a healthy process of spiritual growth. All one has to do is read the Gospels to see that Jesus welcomed questions and participated in healthy debate. This is one way that Jesus made disciples. Yet many churches stunt discipleship because of their desire to control what their congregants believe, and in doing so, they inadvertently quench the Holy Spirit from working in the hearts of their people. This is one reason that many young people are leaving churches that are governed by a climate of fear and control. We need to recognize that having questions is a humble act of worship. It is an acknowledgment of how limited our minds are in comprehending the greatness of God. A questioning and humble spirit can be a powerful form of worship and a transformative way that we give God glory and praise. Yet those who sincerely ask questions are far too often labeled heretics. For years, the religious establishment has often used this word to control people and to dispel any form of questioning.[12] However, the proper definition of heretic is not someone who challenges secondary theological stances. Rather, a heretic is someone with a divisive spirit who too easily cuts off people who challenge their own convictions. The one who divides the body of Christ is the heretic, not the one who has questions.

I love the great commission story in Matthew 28, when the disciples meet the risen Jesus. Matthew writes in verse 17 that "when they saw him, they worshiped him; but some doubted." These followers of Jesus, his loyal disciples, had spent time with Jesus and were present when he was arrested, tortured, and crucified. After the resurrection Jesus appeared to them, and in this story, we see them with Jesus once again. Yet some of them doubted! How could this be?

As strange as their doubt might be, we come across something that seems even more surprising. Jesus does not say a single word about their doubt. He doesn't struggle with the fact that some of his disciples are experiencing questions concerning him. In fact, Jesus seems to ignore their doubts as he commissions all of them, including those who doubted, to go into the world as his emissaries. Apparently, Jesus has no problems with doubters among his ranks and does not see doubt as a disqualifying factor for following him or even for receiving a call to ministry.

Perhaps one of the reasons Jesus never worried about people who doubted was because he accepted doubts as a normal part of the Christian life. In fact, Jesus most likely knew that the Holy Spirit was at work in these doubters' lives, and that their uncertainties were one of the most powerful ways that they would grow in their faith. So if you find yourself experiencing a degree of fear because of your doubts, know that Jesus has not rejected you. Doubts and questions are good and normal. They are how we grow!

Do not be afraid to struggle with what the Bible teaches or to ask questions. This is one of the key ways we develop a deeper faith. Like Jacob, we must be prepared to wrestle with God.[13] To avoid this "wrestling with God" is to live a false life and relinquish a foundational piece of growing in faith. It is in the wrestling with our beliefs that we develop our spiritual muscles. However, when we are too afraid to grapple over what we believe, we avoid the struggle and tap out in our spiritual growth, surrendering to fear. The church should be a wrestling ring where warriors are welcome to work out their faith with fear and trembling.[14] Accept this book as part of your training regimen in developing strong faith muscles. This doesn't mean you have to agree with everything written in this book. But if you allow yourself, even in your disagreement you will grow spiritually through wrestling with this book's contents and the accompanying Scriptures. Remember, wisdom is found in struggling with the Bible. In fact, this is truly what it means to meditate on Scripture.

For those of you who are growing weary in your faith, this book can provide the hope you need. Perhaps the questions you have been facing seem to be too much for you, and you are about to throw in the towel and give up on your faith. Maybe you are bloodied, down for the count, and the referee is about to count you out. My prayer is that this book will give you the strength you need to get back up off the canvas. Take heart, my friend, the battle is not over. God's love is real.

Some of you will get excited by this book, while others will heartily disagree with its contents. In either case, take on the beautiful spirit of humility, knowing that God speaks to those who are humble of heart. "He guides the humble in what is right and teaches them his way" (Psalm 25:9).

I have included discussion questions at the end of each chapter for individual study you can use with small groups or a house church. Feel free to share what you are reading with others, but do so clothed with compassion, kindness, humility, gentleness, and patience (Colossians 3:12). There is no heresy in this book—just great discussion points that drive us to God's Scripture. Above all else, pray for the Spirit to teach you the love of God revealed both in Jesus Christ and the Bible.

Just as my father set out on his journey to a strange and distant shore, I welcome you aboard for this great spiritual journey. Rather than a suitcase, bring your Bible along with you. You will need it. Be prepared to leave behind the comforts of life in a familiar port to travel through some rough waters, but have confidence in the captain of our ship. God knows exactly where he is taking you.

God bless,
Colin McCartney

PART ONE

GOD LOVES YOU

God loves you.
He's on your side.
He's coming after you.
He's relentless.

—LEIF PETERSON,
eulogy for his father, Eugene Peterson

ONE

Does God Love You or Just Tolerate You?

EACH YEAR MY CITY HOSTS the Toronto International Film Festival, affectionately known as TIFF, one of the world's most attended film festivals. Every September, around half a million film enthusiasts flood the streets of Toronto over a period of eleven days to watch approximately four hundred movie screenings in theaters across the city. TIFF is one of the most influential film festivals in the world, bringing many of Hollywood's biggest stars together to help create Oscar buzz. During TIFF, it is not uncommon to bump into famous actors on the streets or in local hotels, restaurants, and coffee shops. For those who love films and all that goes with them, "Hollywood North" is the place to be at this time of year.

I love TIFF and the joy it brings to my city. Strangely enough, one of the things I enjoy the most about the film festival is waiting in long lines to get into world premieres. Usually waiting in line is not my idea of a fun time, but at TIFF, it is a different experience. This is especially the case when I am with my friend Steve, who is a bit of a Hollywood insider thanks to his access to the directors, producers, and actors present at the festival through his growing media platform with Screenfish. Steve insightfully understands that movies are the language of our culture that can often bring us into a space that exposes our souls to longings and desires we might not even be aware of or even know we have or need. This is the power of film, and it's why movies are so important to my friend and to all the people in our line waiting to enter a theater during TIFF. While waiting in these long lines, I witness something spectacular—a sea of strangers become bonded together by the spirit of film. It's like a huge family reunion taking place right before my eyes. In the safety of this type of community, it is a common occurrence for complete strangers to become vulnerable and share stories of how specific movies have affected their lives. I experience God among these strangers as we are connected by the yearning of our souls expressed through the unifying expression of film. When this happens, I realize I am on sacred ground.

TIFF truly creates a divine joy in our city each year, and that is why I will never forget one fateful day when, for a short time, my experience of TIFF was robbed of the happiness it brings. While walking down a street to attend a promotional event for the 2016 civil rights–era movie *Hidden Figures*, I came across a crowd of irritated festival attendees. At first, I didn't know what was happening, but it was obvious that something was wrong. I could feel a strong sense of negative energy just ahead and a palpable presence of something evil. Goosebumps ran up and down my arms and my skin began to crawl. I could feel tension in the air as I saw visibly upset people walking toward me. Some were shaking their heads, others were shouting, but most were simply walking away from the source of this tension as quickly as possible. I looked for the cause of this irritation and was shocked to see a group of very angry Christians who, in their confused minds, were trying to evangelize people attending TIFF. These street preachers were decked out in shirts with the words "Fear God" emblazoned on the front, and were brandishing large banners condemning people to hell. They took aim at everyone and everything in their path, yelling their fiery message about a vengeful, wrathful God without any hint of compassion in their voices. I heard some festivalgoers muttering under their breath that they hate Christians as they walked away from these overzealous proselytizers in disgust. Like the people who directly experienced their vitriol, I felt violated by these uncaring outsiders who had selfishly desecrated the joy among all of us at TIFF that day. Their approach was very different from the caring two-way conversations I had with people in those long movie lines as we listened to each other share stories that often contained elements of the love of God magnified through film. The message of God's love was not present here, though, not now, not on this street corner. Instead of hearing about a God who loves them, people were running away from a message about a God who hates them. I was heartbroken, and immediately went into damage-control mode, speaking to as many strangers as possible, pleading with them to believe that God is not at all like the deity this group proclaimed. But what could I do? The street preachers had megaphones and I didn't. I was outnumbered by this motley crew of toxic Christians.

When I shared this negative experience with a close friend of mine, I was surprised by his response; "Their method might be wrong, but their message is right. God is angry with us because we have sinned against a holy God."

In speaking to other Christians I know, I discovered that most of them also had similar responses. They dismissed the methodology of this group of judgmental proselytizers as over the top, but grudgingly affirmed that their theology of an angry God is correct. Could this be true? Could my friends be right in supporting the message of these extremists? Is our holy God actually angry with sinful humanity? Should we fear God, just as this group told us to? And if their message is true, what does that tell us about God?

While reflecting on my experience with these angry Christians, I couldn't help but think of the famous sermon entitled "Sinners in the Hands of an Angry God," preached by eighteenth-century revivalist Jonathan Edwards,[1] and recognized as one of the greatest sermons ever delivered. I remember that, as a new Christian, I loved every word of it. It is said that when Jonathan Edwards preached this sermon, he could not finish his message because of the shrieking, crying, and weeping among the audience. One of the most famous lines of his sermon is this passionate description of what God is like: "The God that holds you over the pit of hell, much in the same way as one holds a spider, or some loathsome insect, over the fire, abhors you, and is dreadfully provoked; His wrath towards you burns like fire; he looks upon you as worthy of nothing else but to be cast into the fire; He is of purer eyes than to bear to have you in His sight; you are ten thousand times more abominable in His eyes than the most hateful venomous serpent is in ours."[2]

Is this a true depiction of God's view of us? Does God really abhor us? Does God look at a newborn baby and see her as an abomination? According to Jonathan Edwards, that is exactly how God sees all humanity, and how God sees you and me.

Many Christians believe in Jonathan Edwards' view of an angry God. I once believed in this view of God as well. I was taught by my church that an all-holy God cannot be in the presence of unholy people. Like many Christians, I believed that God is too pure and righteous to bear the presence of sinners like me. Sadly, this message of an angry and spiteful God is very common in many Christian circles. One famous Bible teacher, when asked if he believed in the well-known statement "God loves the sinner but hates the sin," responded by saying, "It is just not true to give the impression that God doesn't hate sinners by saying he loves the sinner and hates the sin. He does hate sinners. His wrath is real. It is not something he pours out on people he approves of. This infinite disapproval is what the Bible means when it says God hates sinners. He infinitely disapproves of them."[3]

Later in his talk, this same Bible teacher went on to say, "Sins do not suffer in hell; sinners suffer in hell. I wonder what people who say that believe about hell, because he is not punishing sin in hell, he is punishing sinners in hell. He hates—now here is the paradox—and he loves at the same time. For God so loved the world that he hates. Hate and love are simultaneous as God looks upon hateful, rebellious, corrupt, loathsome, wicked God-dishonoring sinners."[4]

According to this popular Christian leader, God hates every one of us with an infinite disapproval and is eternally upset with us. Furthermore, this Bible teacher believes that we are all loathsome creatures in God's eyes, and that God has a love-hate relationship with the world, in which God hates each of us individually but loves us corporately.[5] This brings up many questions: Is it possible to eternally hate someone, yet also love them at the same time? Can two complete opposites, such as hate and love, exist simultaneously in God? Is it even possible to combine these two opposing mindsets in order to experience loving hatred toward a person?

Some of you reading this, especially those of you who have a more positive image of God, may think that I am overexaggerating the problem of negative portrayals of God by picking and choosing the most extreme examples. This is not the case. In fact, a national study conducted by Baylor University asked how people in the United States view God.[6] Only 23 percent of respondents saw God as benevolent or loving, while 32 percent viewed God as authoritarian, willing to punish people for ungodly acts, including through using earthquakes and other forms of natural disasters to wreak his vengeance. Sixteen percent viewed God as critical, holding an unfavorable assessment of humanity, and 24 percent saw God as distant and uninvolved with life. Atheists made up for the other 5 percent. This means that a whopping 77 percent of Americans see God in a negative light, as authoritarian, critical, distant, or nonexistent!

These kinds of statistics are fuel on the fire for the new atheists, providing them with the fodder they need to energize their arguments.[7] They cleverly argue that if our image of God is of a deity who is perpetually upset with us, then this belief can only result in a terribly pessimistic self-image. This extremely negative view of oneself will also infect a person's perception of others, so that they are seen in a similarly harmful light. The outcome is disastrous in so many ways. This is especially true in religious circles. If we believe that the world is being overrun by hopeless sinners and governed by a God who is upset with us, what hope do we have for a better future?

This miserable concept of God, accompanied by an abject view of ourselves, can only breed further contempt toward others. This is why it appears that the more fundamentalist a religion becomes, the more intolerant it is toward fellow human beings. If humanity is as loathsome to God as many religious leaders claim, then it's not a big jump to believe that human life does not hold much value. If this is the case, why not drop bombs on fellow human beings, especially if their religion is not the true one? Why waste time being involved in social justice? Or why care about the environment if everything is going to go up in smoke in the end? Why be concerned about global warming if humanity is hopelessly broken, and God is about to smite the cosmos? Is it any wonder why so many believers caught up in this unbearable theology seem to hold no concern for the future state of our planet? If Mother Earth is sinking deeper and deeper into the ocean of sin, why bother trying to make things better?

To many, attempting to make the world a better place is like rearranging deck chairs on the *Titanic* while the whole ship is going down. Why bother? In this theology, things cannot get better; they can only get progressively worse until Jesus returns. Since this is the case, why waste time trying to make a dying world a better place when you can hunker down and await the second coming of a wrath-filled Christ? Many Christians provide an abundance of reasons, including these, for the new atheists to vehemently oppose religion. Can we really blame these skeptics for their opposition to such a negative, self-defeating, unloving, globally damaging worldview?

For most of my life I struggled with the nagging feeling that I never was able to measure up to God's expectations. I was taught that I was an enemy of God because I was a sinful reprobate. This negative view of myself and of God affected me in some very damaging ways. I tried my best to live a life that pleased an angry God, and this exhausted me. After all, I believed that I was born a sinner, which meant I was hated by God. Even if God did try to love me, I felt that his love was an obligation, and not freely given. My religion taught that God loved me only because Jesus took the punishment that I deserved from a very displeased God. Thanks to Jesus taking a solid beating from God on my behalf, God was now required to love me.[8] Through the cross, Jesus put God between a rock and a hard place, forcing God to pour out his wrath on the innocent Jesus instead of on the truly guilty one—me. As a result, God was forced to love me, even if my unholy state still ticked him off. Viewing your salvation in this light completely messes up your self-image and worldview while making you live a life of great shame.

The effects of this form of forced love can be seen in some families. I know people who have never known their birth father or mother. In many cases, these people were fortunate enough to have a wonderful stepparent enter their lives and love them as if they were their own child. In this familial environment, stepchildren grow into secure and healthy individuals. However, I also know of some very sad situations in which a stepparent took in children whom they never really loved. The stepparent felt obligated to love the stepchildren only because of the love for the child's birth mother or father. In these cases, even if the stepparent said they loved the stepchildren, the children knew that this love was just words, and that it was a sham. When it came to a life-giving relationship with the stepparent, something was lacking—a truly transformative love that says, "You are valuable and important to me." In these unhealthy family relationships, many stepchildren grow up to become unfulfilled, insecure adults, exhausted by trying to gain the missing love of the unloving stepparent.

This is exactly what happens when we believe that God is obliged to love us because of his love for his Son. In this belief system, God is like a stepfather who is grudgingly forced to love us, his new stepchildren. It's as if Jesus said from the cross, "If you love me, Father, you will love my children."

In this scenario, God's love is coerced because he owes it to Jesus to love us. But true love cannot be coerced. True love comes from the heart, not just the mind. Many unloved stepchildren are walking examples of this truth.

Unfortunately, it seems that many churches are full of unloved stepchildren forced to live in a dysfunctional family. This is because many in the church have a twisted image of God as an irritated stepparent who is obligated to love us. To make matters worse, many of us view God as a stepparent with anger management issues. It's as if God holds a deep hatred toward us, brought on by his constant state of disapproval because we never measure up to his holy expectations. Those who believe this find themselves always running to Jesus for protection from God. This is a textbook example of a dysfunctional family. Unfortunately, this is the state of many individuals and churches today.

I remember being told that because I accepted Jesus as my Savior, God no longer sees me as my bad sinful self, but instead only sees Jesus in my place. I have come to realize how dangerous this concept is, because it assumes that humanity is worthless, nothing but sinful trash that deserves to be burned up in God's fiery wrath. In this understanding, Jesus stands between degenerate sinners and God, deflecting God's wrath by taking it upon himself on our behalf so that we won't face the judgment of a so-called loving God. This is what I was taught: Jesus had protected me, the sinner, from God's wrath, and if it wasn't for Jesus, I would be dead! The problem with this belief is that it is not mentioned in the Bible.[9] And on a more practical level, it has horrible repercussions for our self-esteem, as well as for how we act toward others. If we believe we have no value before God, then how can we ever value the worth of others? If we believe Jesus shields us from God pouring out his wrath upon us, then how can we ever love ourselves enough to show love to others who do not believe as we do, and therefore are not shielded by Jesus?

A fear-based religion that exalts the glory of God by em-phasizing the worthlessness of humanity is not a very good foundation to build your life upon. Yet this type of theology has become the norm in far too many Western churches, sem-inaries, and denominations. It breeds great shame in people to think that they can never, ever please a God who is perpetually angry with them for being sinners. To believe that God hates us but loves us at the same time—if that is even possible—is a very difficult burden to bear, one that inevitably breeds a performance-based faith, which drives us to live a works-based Christianity in an attempt to make God happy with us. For me, this meant doing all the right religious stuff—church at-tendance, Bible reading, prayer, lots of good works in ministry —all while experiencing a ton of guilt. My subconscious view of this angry and eternally disappointed God who was forced to tolerate me because of Jesus drove me into an exhausting life of trying to make God happy with me. Each time I failed, each time I committed sin and did not measure up to God's standard, I felt great shame with God's disappointment in me. As a result, I had to work harder, day in and day out, to perform an exhausting religious dance that could never end well.

Believing in a perpetually angry God is like carrying the burden of Sisyphus. According to Greek mythology, Sisyphus was punished by the gods, who forced him, for all eternity, to push a heavy boulder up a hill, only to have it come rolling back down each time he got close to the top. I know how Sisyphus must have felt, because I was Sisyphus, and the boulder was my belief in a disapproving and angry God who could never be pleased by all my hard work. The more I tried to make God happy, the heavier the boulder felt on my shoulders, a burden too much for me to bear. My life always came crashing down, only for me to take the boulder back and push harder. How could I possibly live a life of peace with myself and others if God was always upset with me? It was a heavy burden to bear, but I never stopped trying to keep pushing that boulder back up the hill . . . every time, I pushed, grunting and sweating nonstop, until I was exhausted. It was a true punishment and a horrible way to live.

But what if God is not like this? What if God has never rejected us, regardless of what we do? How would life be different if the love and acceptance we see in Jesus are an exact reflection of the love and acceptance God the Father has always and eternally had toward us, and has toward us even right now? What if God never needed Jesus to be his whipping boy for us, because he continuously loved us all along, even before the cross? Now that is truly good news. In fact, it is the gospel.

QUESTIONS TO DISCUSS
Read Acts 17:16-34

1. Were there any "lightbulb" moments that struck you as being very important from this chapter? If yes, why were they important to you?

2. Share examples of how you have seen God reveal himself to us in popular culture.

3. If the apostle Paul were at TIFF, would he act like the angry proselytizers I described? Why do you feel this way?

4. How did Paul portray God to the Athenians?

5. Why do you think most people have a negative view of God?

6. Can God love and hate people at the same time? Explain the reasoning for the answer you give. Can love and hate coexist? If yes, then how does this relate to God and us? If no, then how does this relate to God and us?

7. What are some ways that Christians give atheists fuel for their fire?

8. Have you ever felt like Sisyphus? Explain your answer.

9. What is one thing you will do this week in light of what you learned from this discussion?

TWO

Why We Need to Believe in a God of Love

WHAT DO YOU THINK ABOUT GOD? The answer to this question is vital, not only for your spiritual well-being, but also for your mental and physical health. Before you read this chapter, please find a quiet place to think. Have a pen and paper handy, and feel free to grab a cup of coffee. Prepare to spend time in uninterrupted silence so you can thoughtfully and honestly write about how you view God. Although God is an interdependent Trinity, try to focus on how you envision God the Father separately from Jesus the Son and from the Holy Spirit. Take your time while doing this. Be rigorous and detailed, and allow yourself to go deep into your subconscious to find out what you truly believe about God. Ask yourself the following questions as a guide:

- When you think of the stories you have read or heard about God from the Old Testament, what is the image of God that comes to your mind?

- How has God been portrayed to you in the religious education you received or are currently receiving from your church or from people close to you?

- Is God upset with you? With the world? If yes, how does God deal with his displeasure?

- Is God ever absent or distant, or is God always nearby?

- Does God smile on you only when you are good, or is God always pleased with you no matter what you do?

Allowing yourself to go deep into your soul to answer these questions will tell you a lot about how you view God.

The way that we imagine God is vital for the health of our personal well-being, as it affects how we interact with ourselves and the world around us. As A. W. Tozer has stated,

> What comes into our minds when we think about God is the most important thing about us. For this reason, the gravest question before the Church is always God Himself, and the most portentous fact about any man is not what he at a given time may say or do, but what he in his deep heart conceives God to be like. We tend by a secret law of the soul to move toward our mental image of God. This is true not only of the individual Christian, but of the company of Christians that composes the Church. Always the most revealing thing about the Church is her idea of God.[1]

A negative view of God is very harmful. Simply put, a fear-based spirituality can only result in feelings of inadequacy, guilt, and shame that result from feeling that we never measure up to who God wants us to be. The fruit of such a theology is rotten to the core.

In preparing the way for Jesus, John the Baptist spoke these very strong words about beliefs that produce bad fruit: "The ax is already at the root of the trees, and every tree that does not produce good fruit will be cut down and thrown into the fire" (Matthew 3:10).

When we read the full text of Matthew 3, it becomes clear that Jesus is the ax about which John the Baptist spoke. Immediately after John speaks about one who brings judgment, Jesus appears on the scene, fulfilling the Baptizer's words.[2] For the rest of Jesus' ministry, we clearly see him at work as the ax, challenging the religious establishment's futile teachings and cutting down their fruitless beliefs. Each word and action of Jesus is like a perfectly placed blow of an ax swung right to the heart of one specific faulty teaching that oppressed and divided God's children. This major false teaching that so incensed Jesus was the harmful portrayal of God as unapproachable and full of hostility toward sinful humanity.

Time and time again, we see Jesus openly defying the lie that God's favor could be expressed only when his children kept religious laws so that God could grudgingly accept them. We see this ax at work in the way that Jesus loved and embraced those whom the religious leaders believed were rejected by God as sinners. Each sinner-filled party that Jesus attended was a massive blow to the tree representing a spiteful God. Throughout the Gospels, we watch the splinters fly as Jesus befriends those whom the religious elite have labeled unclean, and whenever he heals a leper or a person who is lame. The bright gleam of the ax flashes each time Jesus welcomes an adulterous woman, a tax collector, or a rejected Samaritan.

All of this gets Jesus into trouble, but he doesn't stop swinging his ax, and he even goes after the very roots of the false teachings about a spite-filled God when he confronts the teachers of the law and the Pharisees. Jesus doesn't mince words with these religious elites. He ferociously cuts into their character like a skilled axman, publicly calling them out as hypocrites, children of hell, and snakes (see Matthew 23). One of the few times we see Jesus clearly angry with anyone is when he confronts these religious leaders concerning their ostracizing view of a hostile, unwelcoming, petty God. "Be careful," Jesus warns. "Watch out for the yeast of the Pharisees" (Mark 8:15).

Jesus' warning about the teaching of the Pharisees is as meaningful for followers of Jesus today as it was for his original disciples. Two thousand years later, the yeast of the Pharisees continues to work its way through the church, embedding itself into our views of God. Many pastors teach about a vengeful God who cannot stand being in the presence of sinners, a message that sounds very similar to the one Jesus stood against. These toxic teachings need to be chopped down at their roots and thrown into the fire. They are trees that do not produce good fruit. They stand in complete opposition of the teachings and life of Jesus.

In stark opposition to this false, fear-based image of God, Jesus lived and taught the truth that God has a never-ending abundance of love for every one of us, every second of every day of our lives, no matter what we do, think, or say. No matter what stage of life you are in, young or old, rich or poor, single, married, or divorced, sick or well, free or in prison—God is deeply in love with you because God is love (1 John 4:16). To believe anything different from what Jesus modeled and taught about God is not only wrong but, as you will soon find out, dangerous.

THE IMPORTANCE OF HAVING A LOVING CONCEPT OF GOD

What we think about God affects our brain

What we think about God matters greatly. Recent developments in brain science point to the impact that our image of God has on our lives and the lives of those around us. A loving or negative view of God rewires our brain in positive or harmful ways. Brain science has demonstrated that what we believe about God has the power to change our brain structure in a way that will either bring us life or death!

Christian psychiatrist Timothy Jennings shares his expertise in brain science, explaining how our view of God affects our brain for better or worse.

> Recent brain research . . . has documented that all forms of contemplative meditation were associated with positive brain changes—but the greatest improvements occurred when participants meditated specifically on a God of love. Such meditation was associated with growth in the prefrontal cortex (the part of the brain behind our forehead where we reason, make judgements and experience Godlike love) and subsequent increased capacity for empathy, sympathy, compassion and altruism. But here's the most astonishing part. Not only does other-centered love increase when we worship a God of love, but sharp thinking and memory improve as well. In other words, worshipping a God of love actually stimulates the brain to heal and grow.
>
> However, when we worship a god other than one of love—a being who is punitive, authoritarian, critical or distant—fear circuits are activated and if not calmed, will result in chronic inflammation and damage to both brain and body. As we bow before authoritarian gods, our characters are slowly changed to be less like Jesus.[3]

Note that Jennings states that when our fear circuits are constantly activated, we will get sick in both brain and body. In other words, an authoritarian view of God will actually cause brain damage because of the constant bombardment of fear and anxiety flooding the believer's mind. Knowing this helps me understand the dysfunctional behavior of the angry Christians I ran into at the Toronto International Film Festival, as described in the previous chapter. This also helps explain why religious fundamentalists even go so far as to murder people in the name of God. To put it simply, they have brain damage that has resulted from the poison produced by their toxic image of God.

As you can see, there is much at stake when it comes to how we view God.

What we think about God affects our relationship with God

Not only does our view of God affect our brain and shape our behavior, but it also affects our relationship with God. To put it succinctly, how can we ever approach God or even think of building a relationship with God if we believe God is always upset with us? The natural and safe way to deal with easily angered people is to avoid them at all costs. No one wants to be in the presence of these types of people, and if this is the case, who would ever want to be in the presence of a God of eternal anger?

It is impossible to have a healthy relationship built on fear. It just doesn't work. None of us can possibly have a fruitful relationship with someone we feel can lash out at us at any minute. John makes the life-giving declaration that "God is love. Whoever lives in love lives in God, and God in them. This is how love is made complete among us so that we will have confidence on the day of judgment: In this world we are like Jesus.

There is no fear in love. But perfect love drives out fear, because fear has to do with punishment. The one who fears is not made perfect in love" (1 John 4:16-18).

God is love. What wonderful news. What healing words. What an incredible, life-affirming fact. Never forget these three words—God is love—because these three words are the fuel that energizes a healthy, life-giving, day-to-day relationship with God. John's simple equation about God is very significant:

God is love + God is perfect = perfect love

God's love is perfect love, and as John reminds us, perfect love drives out fear, because fear has to do with punishment. It is because of God's love that we can approach God in full confidence that he won't lash out at us in vengeful anger.

In Hebrews 12:5-6 we read, "And have you completely forgotten this word of encouragement that addresses you as a father addresses his son? It says, 'My son, do not make light of the Lord's discipline, and do not lose heart when he rebukes you, because the Lord disciplines the one he loves.'"

Later we read, "God disciplines us for our good, in order that we may share in his holiness. No discipline seems pleasant at the time, but painful. Later on, however, it produces a harvest of righteousness and peace for those who have been trained by it" (Hebrews 12:10-11).

The writer of Hebrews never uses the word *punishment* in describing how God treats his children. The word he uses is *discipline*, which is very different from punishment. Punishment has no redeeming quality. It has to do with retribution and hurting someone because they have done something wrong. However, discipline is different. It has to do with restoring someone and rebuilding character. To fail to discipline your child is an act of neglect. To punish your child is abuse. To discipline your child is to love her because discipline is meant to restore and benefit the one who needs it. Punishment produces anger, fear, and all forms of negative behavior, but discipline "produces a harvest of righteousness and peace for those who have been trained by it."

Jesus understood how important it is for us to understand God as loving so that we can trust him, knowing that he will never turn away from us. Jesus taught that God is like a loving father who unconditionally accepts his wayward prodigal children back into his family by hosting a welcome home party![4] Jesus describes God as a perfectly loving father by using the Aramaic word *Abba* (see Mark 14:36). This word *Abba* actually means "daddy." It was an affectionate expression used by a beloved child in a loving relationship with his father. Imagine a doting father arriving home from an extended trip. As he walks through the door, he is tackled by his little daughter, who runs and flings herself into his arms while joyfully exclaiming, "Daddy's home!" In response, this daddy instinctively hugs his child in his strong arms as his heart overflows with love and compassion for his child. I know all about this feeling because this happened to me countless times when my children were young. My heart nearly burst from the love I had, and still have, for my now grown-up children. Our perfect Father is an *Abba* Daddy. He is not angry with his children. How could he? He loves his children with an immeasurable love. This is how Jesus describes God as our Daddy. We can safely be in his presence. We can run to him any time, knowing that his arms are wide open in love for every one of us. Our "Daddy" never turns away from us, never.

The fact that Jesus described God as an *Abba* Daddy to all, and especially to the prodigals who were labeled "sinners" in his day, would have been a shock to his listeners, both Jewish and pagan. The Pharisees and teachers of the law would have considered this to be a blasphemous word to describe God. They believed that God was far too holy to be approached as children would approach their daddy. For them, a holy God could not tolerate unholy people. Temple rites had to be observed and religious rituals kept in order for unholy people to approach a holy God. The Romans also had a fear-based image of their gods, whom they saw as petty, vindictive, and unapproachable. But along comes Jesus, this simple rabbi from Nazareth, proclaiming God as an affectionate daddy who is always, without doubt, deeply in love with each and every one of his children.

God loves you as any good father does, and because of this we can approach him as our heavenly *Abba*.

What we think about God affects our obedience to God

Having a proper image of a loving God will have a powerful influence on our obedience to God. Jesus said, "If you love me, keep my commands. . . . Anyone who loves me will obey my teaching. . . . Anyone who does not love me will not obey my teaching" (John 14:15, 23-24).

It couldn't be said any more clearly—love, not fear, is the great motivation for obedience. Jesus didn't say, "If you fear me, keep my commands," or "Anyone who fears me will obey my teaching." He said that loving him is the power source that enables us to do God's will.

One of the arguments I often hear used against having too large of a view of God's love is that such a view will lead people to go on sinning because they don't fear God. Some people believe that fear is the greatest motivator for righteous living. I used to believe this. I thought that people are driven to accomplish things if they fear the repercussions of failure. In some cases, using fear as a motivation seems to work, but in the rare situations where this might appear to be the case, all one has to do is look closer to see that it never is a successful or long-lasting form of motivation. Not only does fear cause exhaustion as we try to live a life free of rejection, but it also causes us to hurt others to achieve results.

I have seen this worked out in countless situations in the sports my children have played over the years. One coach in particular based her motivation on instilling fear and shame in her players. No matter how well a player did, it was never good enough for this coach. Why? Because this coach believed that her players would get better only if she pushed, shamed, and scared them into perfection. In the eyes of this coach, a player was never good enough and always needed to work harder to be better. Does this sound similar to the way that some people relate to God? We often see God as pushing, shaming, and scaring us into being perfect. It truly is an exhausting way to live.

What I witnessed in this sports team is what happens in far too many churches. A pastor and leadership team who hold to an angry view of God will set standards that the congregants must meet or else they are deemed sinful. This fear-based theology is preached from the pulpit and taught in Sunday school classes, as people are guilted into living a life of religious works instead of focusing on having a loving relationship with their *Abba* God. By doing this, these churches have everything upside down. They believe that obedience must be taught first, before we can love God. But Jesus says, "If you love me, you will obey my commands" (see John 14:23). We need to start with loving Christ first, before obedience. If we reverse the order, it will only result in graceless compliance to rules, which leads to shame, pride, or putting down others who don't meet the mark. This is not a healthy church, but a poisonous one that will inadvertently produce toxic Christians.

The apostle Paul reminds us that God's method to motivate us to live a righteous life does not come from fearing God. "Do you think lightly of the riches of His kindness and restraint and patience, not knowing that the kindness of God leads you to repentance?" (Romans 2:4 NASB). It is God's kindness, not a fear of God's wrath, that leads to repentance.

What we think about God affects the world we live in

It is important to understand that our perceptions help create our world. If we see God as upset with us as sinners deserving God's wrath, then we shape a world that reflects those beliefs.

Rabbi Lord Jonathan Sachs wisely said, "Religion is like fire and like fire it warms, but it also burns. We are the guardians of the flame."[5] A religion can become warming only if we see God as the psalmist does in Psalm 136, as a God whose "love endures forever." Seeing that God possesses an eternal and enduring love for all humanity will help us see the world as a place of hope and purpose, where people are loved forever by God. John sums up why it is important for us to fully grasp the great love God has for each and every person on our planet when he writes, "And so we know and rely on the love God has for us. God is love. Whoever lives in love lives in God, and God in them" (1 John 4:16).

When I think of God's love working in and through us, I envision an endless, love-filled hurricane in which God is the epicenter, radiating out love to those who confidently approach him as *Abba*. We get caught up in God—the eye of this wonderful storm—whose powerful, all-encompassing love whirls in and all around us, propelling us outward to influence others with God's contagious love. It's a glorious image of a God-centered life that is built on a God of love.

If we are to bring the peace of Christ into a peaceless world, we must be swept up into God's loving hurricane. Repentance won't come from a fear of an angry God. People will turn from evil when they have been affected by the winds of love that passionately blow forth from the outstretched arms of *Abba*.

I have seen this hurricane of God's awesome love all around me. A few years ago, I visited friends who serve in a seemingly hopeless *favela*, or slum, in Brazil. My friends are a young couple who met each other after leaving the safety of their own countries to serve as missionaries. They eventually got married and are living in a house with other Brazilian young people. Making your home in the heart of a favela is not an easy thing to do. I know this to be true because my wife and I lived with these friends for only two weeks, and each night we were serenaded with loud music, barking dogs, screaming, and sometimes the sound of gunfire. One night we had a little visitor come join us in our room in the form of a rat. We were touched by the love our friends had for each other, their team, and the people of the favela as we saw the work they were involved in and met other young missionaries serving drug-addicted youth, forgotten children, and abused runaways.

One evening, my wife and I were invited to visit people addicted to crack cocaine in a part of the favela known as Cracolândia, or Crackland. As I recounted in an earlier book, we traveled through sloping narrow streets until we came to a dimly lit road where the van stopped to let us all out. Carrying coffee, juice, and bread, we slowly made our way past gang members who acted as lookouts. When they were satisfied that we were not members of rival gangs or police, they gave us freedom to be approached by the many drug-addicted people who hid in the darkness along the gloomy edges of the street. These gaunt, withered shadow people slowly came toward us, limping and stumbling. Many were mentally ill because of the terrible toll the drugs had taken on their bodies. Some were covered in scabs; others were barely clothed. All of them were dirty, broken, and smelled horribly from living on the streets. As we gave out the bread, coffee, and juice, I was overwhelmed by the knowledge that these people were all precious children of God. . . . God knew each beautiful one of them by name. God heard their cries and he understood the hurt they carried. God knew what had happened to them in the past that drove them to the streets and to the drugs they used to help them numb their pain. God saw each man and woman who had sold themselves for sex in order to get money to buy drugs. And here is the astounding reality of all of this pain—God loves each and every one of these hurting individuals.

While in the middle of this sea of people who were homeless, filthy, and drug addicted, I had a revelation. All of a sudden, I realized that I was on holy ground. As I extended some bread and juice to an emaciated, trembling, balding woman, I heard Jesus whisper, "This is my body that was broken for you and this cup is the new covenant in my blood, which is poured out for you. The bread you give these people is my body broken for them. The coffee and juice you serve my hurting children is my blood that was shed for them."

As I looked all around me, I saw people eating and drinking. Some were praying and others were laughing with my friends as we all unknowingly served the eucharist right there with the poorest of the poor. In Cracolândia, we were all loved by God. It did not matter if we were on drugs or not. All of us were equally sinful yet equally loved by Jesus, who broke his body and shed his blood for each and every one of us. There on those filthy streets filled with despair, I realized that God had made this abandoned part of town holy. Cracolândia was a sacred place.[6]

God's hurricane of love is swirling all around us. His loving winds blow through those who understand that our *Abba* is love. When you get swept up into God's wondrous hurricane of love, desolate places become filled with the winds of hope and life. Deserted plains are filled with streams of living water. Lonely, hurting people are able to experience their sacredness as children of their loving Father. It was there, as I stood on holy ground in the midst of Crackland, surrounded by desperate, drug-addicted people, that I felt *Abba's* presence among his abandoned children and was reminded once again that God is love.

QUESTIONS TO DISCUSS

Read 1 John 4:7-21

1. At the beginning of this chapter you were asked to journal about your current image of God. What did you write? What are the sources for your image of God?

2. In what ways have you seen the "yeast of the Pharisees" (Mark 8:15) work its way into your mind? How have you seen it work through religion?

3. Rabbi Lord Jonathan Sachs was quoted in this chapter as saying, "Religion is like fire and like fire it warms, but it also burns. We are the guardians of the flame." Why do you think Sachs speaks of religion in this manner? What is our responsibility when it comes to our religion?

4. From what you now know about brain science, what are some practical steps you can take to be transformed by the renewal of your mind (Romans 12:2)? While discussing this, make sure that you do not slip into a shame- or fear-based methodology in deepening your love relationship with God.

5. What does it mean to you to know that God is your *Abba* Daddy?

6. God is love + God is perfect = perfect love (1 John 4:7-21). What impact could this equation have on your life, others' lives, and the world?

7. What is one thing you will do this week in light of what you learned from this discussion?

THREE

A Christlike God

IN THE LAST CHAPTER, I asked you to write down your thoughts about your view of God as a way of doing some deep self-discovery. By working through that exercise, you should have been able to detect any negative perceptions you might have of God. With this self-awareness, you can begin the challenging task of reorienting your perception of God to that of a loving God. This is a challenge, because many people have had their brains shaped by a damaging view of God thanks to things they have been taught or life circumstances they have experienced. The good news is that our brain's neuroplasticity provides the opportunity for our minds to be reshaped into a more life-giving affirmative view of God. As we continue to work out this process of renewing our minds, let us try another simple exercise.[1]

Please grab another piece of paper and write down what you think Jesus is like. While you do this, prayerfully work through some of these questions:

- Imagine Jesus is sitting with you right now. What would he tell you concerning his feelings toward you?

- What is the image of Jesus that comes to your mind when you think of his teachings?

- What do you think of Jesus when you consider his torturous death on the cross?

- How do Jesus' actions toward those whom his society rejected—lepers, the poor, tax collectors, women of ill repute, and the sick—influence how you imagine what Jesus is like?

When you finish this brief assignment, compare what you wrote about Jesus with what you wrote about God in the reflection exercise from the previous chapter. Does the way you see Jesus line up with how you see God the Father, or do your perceptions of them vary in personality and character?

Some of us hold an image of God the Father that is totally different from our view of Jesus. We may see God the Father as the bad guy. This is the God who is always looking over his shoulder at us, offended by our actions, and who has no problem judging and causing his wrath to fall upon people. Yet when these same Christians talk about Jesus, they describe a completely different person. Jesus isn't angry with sinners; he loves them. Jesus wants to pour his grace on humanity, not his wrath. Though Jesus is holy, he is still very comfortable being in the presence of sinners. In fact, he parties with them. This Jesus isn't easily offended by sinners, nor does he perceive them as his enemies; instead, Jesus sees sinners as sick people who need a doctor. Many of us have two completely different pictures of what God and Jesus are like. But how can this be, when we consider that Jesus is God in the flesh? Since Jesus is God incarnate, why does he seem to be so different from whom many envision God the Father to be?

The completely different views that so many people have of Jesus and God raises the question, What is God truly like? In a discussion with his disciples, Jesus answered this question and engaged in conversation with Philip. Jesus said,

> "I am the way and the truth and the life. No one comes to the Father except through me. If you really know me, you will know my Father as well. From now on, you do know him and have seen him."
>
> Philip said, "Lord, show us the Father and that will be enough for us."
>
> Jesus answered: "Don't you know me, Philip, even after I have been among you such a long time? Anyone who has seen me has seen the Father. How can you say, 'Show us the Father?' Don't you believe that I am in the Father, and that the Father is in me? The words I say to you I do not speak on my own authority. Rather, it is the Father, living in me, who is doing his work. Believe me when I say that I am in the Father and the Father is in me; or at least believe on the evidence of the works themselves." (John 14:6-11)

Jesus clearly asserts that what you see in him is exactly what God is like. Jesus is pointing to himself and saying, "I am the truth about God." In fact, the Greek word that Jesus uses when he says that he is the truth means "something that was once covered but is now unveiled." So Jesus is saying that he has come to uncover, or unveil, what God is truly like. He goes on to tell Philip that if you know him, you know the Father and that "anyone who has seen me has seen the Father." So what is God like? The answer is simple—God is like Jesus because Jesus is God!

Throughout Jesus' ministry we see Jesus revealing what God is like. Each of his acts of kindness points to a God of love. Jesus' fearless compassion had no boundaries and took no prisoners even when it required him to break religious laws. The wild love of God can never be restricted by religious rules, because in God's eyes any religious law that labels people as being unacceptable to God is wrong. We cannot confine God's love to a few so-called worthy people. We see this in the way that God's love boldly erupts through Jesus whenever he encounters lepers, ignored children, abused women, and poor people who have been rejected by society. His tearing down of racial and gender barriers reveals a God who sees everyone as his beloved children. In fact, the only time we see Jesus get upset is when his love for others is fired up into anger when he encounters people being mistreated. Everything Jesus did revealed a God of great love, and this is what got Jesus into a lot of trouble with the religious elite. In particular, they had a problem with Jesus' popularity among those they labeled as "unclean."

This is why the religious leaders derisively judged Jesus as a friend of sinners. Luke tells us, "Now the tax collectors and sinners were all gathering around to hear Jesus. But the Pharisees and the teachers of the law muttered, 'This man welcomes sinners and eats with them'" (Luke 15:1-2). The Pharisees and teachers of the law thought that being a friend of sinners was a great insult, but for Jesus, being a friend of sinners was a tremendous badge of holy honor. In fact, Jesus proudly declares this when he says, "The Son of Man came eating and drinking, and they say, 'Here is a glutton and a drunkard, a friend of tax collectors and sinners.' But wisdom is proved right by her deeds" (Matthew 11:19).

Jesus defends his loving actions toward the outcasts and sinners as wise deeds. By saying this, he also is implying that the pious hypocrisy of his religious critics is complete foolishness. Jesus is reversing the definition of a fool by stating that those who separate themselves from sinners are fools.

Rather than Jesus claiming that a holy God cannot be in the presence of sin, we find Jesus saying the complete opposite. For Jesus, holiness looks like loving sinners. In fact, Jesus was very comfortable with those whom the religious leaders scorned as being unacceptable, unclean, or unholy. Unlike these pious leaders, Jesus spent so much time with sinners that he was accused of being a glutton and a drunkard. This guilt by association is evidence of the high level of comfort Jesus had with sinners, and it also sheds some light on the type of people with whom Jesus hung out and ate meals. In Jesus' culture, sharing a meal with another person was a sign of social acceptance and deep friendship. By his actions, Jesus was stating that he truly enjoyed being in the presence of his close friends, the sinners.

This comfort level Jesus has with sinners flies in the face of a stream of theology taught by many Christians who believe that God is too holy to be near sinners because of their sin.[2] Sadly, those who hold to this belief have chosen to oppose Jesus by taking the side of the Pharisees and teachers of the law. If they are correct in saying that God is too holy to be near sinners or even look upon sin, then how can we explain Jesus and the sinful company he kept? Jesus was delighted to be known as a friend of sinners, and indicated that God the Father feels the same way toward sinners. He, too, is a friend of sinners.

This welcoming love of sinners was often manifested in Jesus' blatant breaking of religious laws. This was a huge issue for the religious leaders of his day, who believed that their freedom from Rome would be hastened by God if more people obeyed the religious laws. This strict adherence to law overruled any form of compassion and grace toward people. For the religious leaders in Jesus' day, keeping the law was the highest goal. However, for Jesus, love was the highest law, and it overruled any religious laws that got in the way of helping people. For Jesus, loving people had nothing to do with their personal morality or what they believed.

In John 5, we come across an episode where we see Jesus challenging the religious power brokers of his day. This was a common occurrence throughout the ministry of Jesus, as the graceless authority that the religious leaders wielded was constantly threatened by Jesus. In this case, Jesus is found guilty of healing the sick on the Sabbath, which to the religious establishment was a serious infraction of the law. In response to their accusation we read,

> In his defense Jesus said to them, "My Father is always at his work to this very day, and I too am working." For this reason they tried all the more to kill him; not only was he breaking the Sabbath, but he was even calling God his own Father, making himself equal with God.
>
> Jesus gave them this answer: "Very truly I tell you, the Son can do nothing by himself; he can do only what he sees his Father doing, because whatever the Father does the Son also does. For the Father loves the Son and shows him all he does." (John 5:17-20)

Jesus can "do only what he sees his Father doing." This means that every single thing he does—eating and drinking with sinners, healing the sick on the Sabbath, accepting sex workers, loving the poor and oppressed, giving grace to Samaritans and Roman oppressors—comes from his Father. This claim bothered the religious elite greatly.

In my city, there is a group of young people who have a heart for women who are involved in the sex trade. Each week they go to places where sex workers ply their trade and hand out homemade cookies or give them roses while telling them that God loves them. This is commendable, and I admire these young people for doing this. In no way do I want to belittle what they are doing. May God bless them and work through them as they seek to show God's love to hurting young women.

Yet I have a sneaking feeling that Jesus would ramp their compassion up a few notches. Instead of handing out flowers or cookies, I believe Jesus would rent a room and talk to these women. He would enjoy their company as his friends, hear their pain, and bring their hearts some healing by being present to them in the midst of their misery while communicating their worth to them as best he could. I am sure this is exactly what the street missionaries are trying to do through their flowers and cookies. I am also sure that some of these missionaries, if not all of them, would be upset with Jesus if they came across him every night while they were giving out cookies and roses. I know I would feel disgusted if this same man was always bringing women into skanky motel rooms and leaving, arm in arm, smiling with them on the way out. By all appearances, Jesus would look like a typical client or procurer, victimizing young women. But here is the catch. Friends of sinners really do not care one bit what their actions might look like to outsiders. Those who commit scandalous acts of grace don't give a rip about appearances or how their behavior might be perceived by those in the religious establishment. This is what it means to be holy by being a friend of sinners, and this is what love does. Loving actions are often shocking in the eyes of others.

I have a friend who is a very well-known Christian leader and speaker. He is so in love with God that, like Jesus, he doesn't care what others think of him. His love for the poor and oppressed often causes him to disregard any form of decorum in order to help people out. One time, he was in Haiti and was staying in a hotel that was also a popular place for teenage sex workers to ply their trade.[3] Sadly, driven by poverty, these teenage girls are forced to find clients whom they can sleep with for a few bucks. Each night my friend would pass by the same three very young girls who stood by the front doors of his hotel. Before he went to bed, he would pray for them. One night as he passed by them, he felt the Holy Spirit tell him to invite them to spend the night in his hotel room. So my friend approached these youngsters and told them he wanted their services for the entire night. Upon giving them his room number, he asked that they come up in fifteen minutes. This gave him enough time to quickly run to his room and order Walt Disney movies to be shown on his television. He also called room service to ask them to bring up all sorts of food for the girls. Shortly thereafter, a quiet knock was heard on his door, and the girls entered his room. He had them make themselves comfortable on his bed in front of the television and began to show them the first Walt Disney movie of the evening. Room service showed up and the girls filled their hungry little bellies with all sorts of food, topped off by four large sundaes. By the time they finished eating, sometime during the second movie, these girls fell asleep. My friend looked at these girls sleeping in the safety of his room and he cried out to God, "What good is this? Here I am giving these children the time of their lives, but tomorrow they will be back outside selling their little bodies to filthy men. Nothing has changed for them, not one thing!"

It was then that my friend heard the Spirit of God speak to him, "But for one night. For one night you gave them back their childhood. For one night you let them be kids again. For one night you let them be children once more. You didn't solve the problems of their lives. But you did what you could. You did what you could."

Could you imagine what would happen if someone had recognized my friend and seen him take three teen sex workers to his room for the night? It would have discredited his ministry and brought shame on his family and himself. It would have caused my friend to lose his ministry. In short, it would have been a huge scandal! But he didn't care. His love for God caused him to have an outrageous love for people.

I tell you this story because this is exactly the kind of thing Jesus did! He had scandalous love. He had no concern for his reputation even if he was labeled a drunkard and glutton and a friend of tax collectors and sinners because of the people with whom he hung out (see Matthew 11:19). Jesus didn't care how he was perceived by those who watched in disgust when a woman whom Jesus knew burst into a VIP dinner hosted by a religious leader. Can you imagine the commotion it caused when she fell before Jesus, weeping and kissing his feet and pouring her perfume on them? The host was offended with how Jesus responded to the woman, and we read that the host thought to himself, "If this man were a prophet, he would know who is touching him and what kind of woman she is—that she is a sinner" (Luke 7:39). A woman doing such a thing to a rabbi was an outrageous, unholy act for sure, but Jesus loved every second of it, because holiness looks like scandalous love.

What Jesus does, God does. When you see Jesus, you see God. God is a scandalous lover of sinful humanity, as is seen in Jesus' perfect unity with God's will. He sees only what the Father shows him, and does what the Father does through him. Jesus' actions are God's actions. Everything we see about Jesus is true about God. How can it not be? As Jesus told his religious adversaries, "You do not know me or my Father. . . . If you knew me, you would know my Father also" (John 8:19).

Jesus is saying that he is the mirror image of God the Father. Jesus is God in the flesh.

Whose opinion do you trust the most concerning what God is like? Do you trust your assumptions about God? Do you allow others' opinions about God to influence you? Are some current religious leaders' views of an angry and spiteful God correct? Or do you trust Jesus' very own words about what he is like, what God is like? Remember what he said: "If you really know me, you will know my Father as well. From now on, you do know him and have seen him. . . . Anyone who has seen me has seen the Father" (John 14:7-9).

The apostle Paul understood the importance of basing our view of God on what we see when looking at Jesus. As Paul writes, "The Son is the image of the invisible God" (Colossians 1:15). Paul goes on to say, "For in Christ all the fullness of the Deity lives in bodily form" (Colossians 2:9). Paul couldn't have made it any clearer. What you see in Jesus is what you see in God. In other words, we have a Christlike God.

The writer of the book of Hebrews says this about Jesus: "The Son is the radiance of God's glory and the exact representation of his being, sustaining all things by his powerful word" (Hebrews 1:3). Jesus exudes God's glory as the precise image of God!

Again, I must ask, what and whom do you trust the most regarding what God is like? Your ideas? Others' opinions? Or Jesus and the apostle Paul?

God has always loved us. It is we who have rejected his love by creating our own stories and beliefs about a wrathful God. God's constant love has been eternally with us all along, but we are the ones who have projected our own anger and violence onto our image of God. As the famous quotation states, "God created man in his own image and man, being a gentleman, returned the favor."[4]

I once heard someone say that we are all like preschool-age children trying to draw our own image of God. We grab some crayons and scribble a picture of what we think God looks like, and then we argue with each other about which picture looks better. Sometimes the argument gets bitter, and one child hits another, or a child sticks his crayon in another youngster's eye. If you read church history, you can see these children fight with one another. But it shouldn't be like this, because during this argument Jesus has already entered the room, declaring that if you have seen him, you have seen God. God is Christlike. God is exactly like Jesus. Yet the fighting continues as people refuse to acknowledge that the only way we can accurately discuss what God is truly like is by beholding Jesus.[5]

It must break God's heart to see himself misunderstood as a wrathful God so unlike the loving God revealed to us by Jesus. God must be greatly saddened when people misrepresent God's character in unloving ways. It must deeply hurt God when he is so badly defamed by Christian proselytizers like the ones who showed up at the Toronto film festival. Their angry words mixed with their judgmental signs were so unlike God, because they did not comprehend that what we see in Jesus is what God is like. We do not want to be guilty of idolatry by impugning the character of God. Yet many today, like the religious leaders in Jesus' day, believe in a false image of an angry God. It is for this reason that Jesus came to prove them wrong and to reveal a more Christlike God. As Richard Rohr writes, summarizing twelfth-century theologian and priest Duns Scotus, "Jesus didn't come to change God's mind about us but to change our mind about God."[6]

Maybe it's time for us to change our mind about God by looking at Jesus?

QUESTIONS TO DISCUSS

Read John 14:6-11

1. Were there any "lightbulb" moments that struck you as being very important from this chapter? If yes, why were they important to you?

2. At the beginning of this chapter you were asked to journal about what your current image of Jesus is like. What did you write? Did it differ from what you wrote about God in the previous chapter?

3. When Jesus says he is the truth (John 14:6), the Greek word used for truth means to "unveil something that was once covered." In what ways has the God of love been covered? In what ways has Jesus unveiled the truth about God?

4. How do you define holiness? How does your definition of holiness fit with the way that Jesus "welcomes sinners and eats with them" (Luke 15:2)?

5. Think through the ways that Jesus exhibited a scandalous love. What would that kind of love look like today?

6. What does this quote mean to you: "Jesus didn't come to change God's mind about us but to change our mind about God"? What are some ways we can help people change their mind about God?

7. What is one thing you will do this week in light of what you learned from this discussion?

FOUR

How God Sees You

IN THE PAST TWO CHAPTERS, I asked you to write about your image of God and about what you think Jesus is like. But what if we were to turn the tables and ask God to write about what he thinks of you? What do you think he would say? What picture do you think God has in his mind each time he thinks of you? This is an important question to ask because our perception of God's view of us directly influences our view of God. For example, if we believe God is upset with us because we have let him down, it is most likely because we believe that God views us with great disappointment or antagonism. A proper understanding of God's view of us is indispensable to a healthy image of God and thus of ourselves.

We have come to see that some of us hold views of Jesus and God that are clearly contradictory. On one hand, we often hear preachers tell us about a God who is deeply offended over sinful humanity and who must judge unrepentant sinners with his holy wrath. On the other hand, we see Jesus proclaiming himself the exact image of the Father God, forgiving and accepting sinners with his open arms of love. So which is it? Is God angered by sin and duty bound to judge sinners? Or is God loving and forgiving, patiently working with sinners to bring them to repentance? Is sin an affront to God, or does God combat sin because it is an affront to his creation? Is God angry at sinners because they sin? Or is God angry at sin because it hurts the sinners God loves?

Can God be forever gracious, yet also full of wrath? Can God be judging and forgiving at the same time? Is any of this even possible?

And how does God view us? The answer to this question is found in the way that God reacts to sinners. "God demonstrates his own love for us in this: While we were still sinners, Christ died for us" (Romans 5:8).

God responds to sinners by loving them and dying for them. Jesus takes our sins upon himself, and receives our wrath, not the Father's anger. His suffering and crucifixion were humanity's doing, not God's. God was never behind the voices that shouted out, "Crucify him!" That's on us. It was our sinful hearts, openly influenced by satanic activity, that cried out for the crucifixion of Jesus. They still do each time we sin. Yet amid all this evil we continue to commit against Jesus, he proclaims forgiveness for us. "Father, forgive them, for they do not know what they are doing" (Luke 23:34). Instead of acting out in vengeance to smite us sinners who crucified his Son, God openly takes our abuse upon himself in loving forgiveness. This is what God's love looks like. This is how much God loves us.

"Father forgive them". These dying words from Jesus' lips were not a desperate plea to the Father in which Jesus begged God to forgive us. They were a statement of agreement among the trinitarian unity of the Father, Son, and Holy Spirit to instantaneously provide forgiveness in response to our sin. "Father, forgive them . . ." is a complete, final statement of utter grace and love. This is how God responds to sinners. How can it be any different? After all, "God did not send his Son into the world to condemn the world, but to save the world through him" (John 3:17). Jesus came not to condemn sinners but to save us.

We can see the value that God places on us when Jesus is caught at a party chock-full of sinners. The religious paparazzi are at the scene and have visual proof that this so-called rabbi of righteousness is partying with the dregs of society. "Now the tax collectors and sinners were all gathering around to hear Jesus. But the Pharisees and the teachers of the law muttered, 'This man welcomes sinners and eats with them'" (Luke 15:1-2).

Caught in the act of welcoming and eating with sinners, Jesus defends himself to his critics by telling three stories to explain his actions. I can only imagine how these religious killjoys reacted to each story Jesus told. Some must have fumed with anger, others most likely squirmed in discomfort, while a few undoubtedly blocked their ears at the heresy they were hearing. Here was Jesus speaking about a God who was not angry with sinners but was desperately in love with them. The God whom Jesus describes and embodies does not despise sinners but values them as precious souls.

God's love toward sinners and the immense value he places on them is seen in each of the stories Jesus shares, but it is the third one—the parable of the prodigal son—that I want to focus on. Here, Jesus audaciously confronts the religious establishment's condemning spirit, driving home the reality of God's great love of sinners. The story (in Luke 15:11-32) revolves around a loving father and his youngest son, who wants his inheritance early so he can leave home. His father sadly relents, and this son proceeds to quickly burn through every dime on loose living. With nothing left, he is forced to return home, broken and humbled by his sin, hoping to be accepted back as a slave. Being from an ancient Middle Eastern culture, he knew that there was no way his father, after being so dishonored, would ever stoop low enough to accept him back as his son. In that culture, fathers must be honored. For a father to welcome back his ungrateful son after such disrespect would be one of the most undignified acts a father could ever allow himself to do. It is clear from this story that Jesus is showing his listeners that this son is representative of the sinners whom Jesus counts as his friends. The very ones he is eating and drinking with in this story.

The other son in the story is ultra-responsible. He is busy trying to do everything he thinks his father wants. One could say that this son's identity is built upon looking good on the outside, especially when he compares himself to his delinquent brother. Yet he is graceless and completely misunderstands what the father truly desires—mercy over sacrifice.[1] Jesus is portraying this older son as just like the religious critics who are confronting him over his love for sinners. Both sons are flawed, but Jesus describes this father as loving both sons equally. This is how much God loves sinners like us.

In each of Jesus' stories, and especially in his story of the prodigal son, Jesus not only defends the value of sinners, but also challenges the negative view of God that was held by too many religious people of his day (and of our day, too). This was a big part of Jesus' ministry, as it was fraught with an ongoing battle between his image of a loving God versus the religious view of an angry God. Through his teachings, his actions, his healings, and yes, even his partying ways, Jesus was boldly declaring that everything religion taught about God was wrong. God is not angry with sinners. God loves sinners.

This message of Jesus—that God is our loving Father—is very important to understand. The good news that God is in love with us is the basis of true Christianity. Unfortunately, this image of God as a loving father has been discounted in many forms of Christianity today. In these sad cases, Christianity falls in line with other religions that portray God with his arms crossed, sneering down at us, while demanding we do things to appease his anger. Jesus exposed this sham of religion by revealing the opposite. According to Jesus, God's arms are not crossed in judgment, but are open wide, seeking desperately to welcome his children. These are the arms of Jesus extended on the cross of Calvary. God has no sneer on his face, and there are no demands placed on us in order to receive his love. He already loves us just as we are.

God does not say, "You better make me happy, or else!" Instead, God says, "I am already happy with you. Just receive my love." God is not an eternally angry God, but an eternally loving God who is for us and not against us. This is the good news, the gospel story. It is the pure Christian faith that is built on Jesus. Yet for so many of us, it is nearly impossible to accept how much we are loved by God.

Concerning this struggle to embrace God's love for us, Brennan Manning writes, "It takes a profound conversion to accept that God is relentlessly tender and compassionate toward us just as we are—not in spite of our sins and faults (that would not be total acceptance), but with them. Though God does not condone or sanction evil, He does not withhold his love because there is evil in us."[2]

It just might take "a profound conversion" for you to accept that God is eternally in love with you. This is probably why Jesus chooses to express God's love for us through a heartwarming story we can feel, instead of using a detached theological argument. Who can't relate to a father's pain in struggling to care for his dysfunctional family as we listen to the story of the prodigal son? Although the son is enormously ungrateful, his father still loves him immensely. When the son embarrasses the family name by wasting all his money on sex, booze, and partying, the father still loves him unceasingly. Instead of rejecting his inconsiderate son or demanding that he prove himself worthy of forgiveness, the father takes him back, no questions asked. This father never rejects his son, but just continues to show him love! He even throws a party for his delinquent son and showers him with gifts, extravagantly showing his love by replacing his son's dirty clothes with a brand-new robe, which was reserved for VIPs only. This sinful, reckless son is the center of attention for his father, and the father celebrates his return by throwing a feast for everyone with a fattened calf. This suggests that when the son left home with his inheritance, his father set aside a calf and made sure that it was overfed in anticipation of his son's returning one day, so that he would have all he needed to throw a sensational welcome home party for his wayward son. Throughout each step of this process, the father displays a never-ending abundance of love toward his errant son.

This is how God views all of us. No matter how badly we mess up, God loves us nonstop. There is no selfish, inconsiderate, hurtful, or immoral activity we could be involved in that can stop God from loving us immeasurably. Thank God he is like the father we read about in the story of the prodigal.

When I think of how the father loved his sons, I am reminded of my own love for my children. As a new parent, I'll never forget the day when my friends had all gathered together in our little home and were being entertained by my infant son. Everything went well until a strange gurgling noise proceeded from my son, followed by a horrible odor. Our son had released one of the worst bowel movements in the history of humanity. The odor was so strong that everyone made a run for the nearest door to escape the stench filling the room. As everyone else ran away from my son, I instinctively ran toward him. Scooping him up in my arms, I quickly whisked him away to another room to change his diaper, which was so soiled that fragments of its contents oozed onto my arms and hands. While I cleaned my son up, I lovingly sang songs to him despite the terrible smell and mess that was all over him and me.

Contrary to what some Christians believe, God's holiness does not cause God to hide out in the corner, fearfully cowering in the presence of sin. Sin is not a form of kryptonite that can defeat God. Jesus is extremely comfortable in the presence of sinners and welcomes them to be his followers. One could even say that while the religious elite ran away from the stench of sinners, Jesus ran toward them with a willing and loving heart to clean them up. Jesus' life makes us reexamine our concept of holiness. In the Old Testament, items were made holy by being set apart for the specific purpose to be used for the worship of God. This is what it means to be holy—to be set apart for worship. Jesus shows us that he, as the holy one, has been set apart to demonstrate love to sinners. In other words, loving sinners is a holy act of worship toward God! With this truth in mind, we must vehemently oppose a petty view of God that claims God is unable to be near sinners. Jesus spends all his time with sinners, and Paul reminds us that God is everywhere, always present, when he writes that "in him we live and move and have our being" (Acts 17:28). Sin doesn't force God to run for cover. The life of Jesus proves that God does not separate himself from sinners because he is too pure to look upon sin. God is the father of all his prodigals, and his arms are eternally opened wide to every one of us sinners.

God's love has no boundaries, but our love can often be restrictive. All throughout this story, even at the end, the sons love their father because of what they can get from him. The younger son repents so he can get a job and food from his father, and the older son works hard so he can get rewarded for his labor. However, this father's love is completely opposite from what we see in his sons. He loves them unconditionally with no benefit to himself. What benefits are there for him to love his sons? The father owns everything, the sons own nothing. The father has all the power, the sons are powerless. The father has the house, the land, and all the money. There is not one benefit to this father to love these sons. Yet the father loves them despite their lack. He loves them warts and all.

We learn something about God here. Just as this father loves his sons unconditionally, so God our Father loves us in the exact same way. There are no benefits for God in loving us, but he loves us anyway. Why is God like this? Why is God always in love with us?

If there was one word to describe who, not what, God is like, what would that word be? The Bible says, "God is love" (1 John 4:16). Love is the one word that describes God's very essence. God eternally loves us. It doesn't matter what we do or how we treat God. God is deeply in love with every one of us. God's love for us is not based on what we can do for God. God just loves us, period. This is divine love, an unconditional and eternal love that never gives up on us.

It is interesting to note that the father never once showed anger toward either of his sons for their behavior. He never punished them. This father understood that if his sons chose to live their lives apart from him, their life choices would be a discipline in and of themselves, teaching them to return to the father's love. This is why the younger son returned home, and it is why he was never punished. His father knew that he had suffered enough and had learned a valuable lesson from his waywardness. In this way Jesus reveals how God disciplines us. Instead of actively pouring out his wrath on us in a punitive manner, God sadly lets us go our way and allows our bad choices to discipline us and lead us to repentance.[3] In the case of the prodigal son we see a father who waits in anticipation for his son to return home. The father is not looking forward for his son to return so he can beat him. The opposite is true. The father is eagerly longing to welcome his son back home so he can bless him.

This father ran toward his son after he saw him from a distance. What does this tell us about this father? The father must have always been gazing out at the horizon, constantly looking to see if his son was coming home. How many days, weeks, and months did this father stare out at the horizon, hoping and praying that today was the day his son would come back home?

In time, the father's dreams and prayers are answered. When his son returns there is no pent-up anger toward the son. It's quite the opposite. Instead of judgment or rage for dishonoring the family name, the father displays extravagant love. Energized by a fullness of compassion toward his wayward son, the old man sprints wildly toward his son and throws himself on him with outstretched arms, hugs, and kisses. What a sight this must have been to see such a tangled, chaotic mess of joy, tears, and laughter.

All throughout this time, the father never demands an apology. He doesn't lecture his son about his irresponsibility. He doesn't pass judgment or punish the son for his sin and rebellion. He just throws an incredible party with food, fine wine, music, and dancing for his child who has come home.

This is how your Father, *Abba*, Daddy God sees every sinner. This is why Jesus loved being in the company of sinners, and it is why he delighted in being a friend of sinners. Most importantly, this is Jesus describing how God sees each and every one of us. God is not disgusted by us, he is in love with us. He is not repelled by our sin but is drawn to us because of our sin. God is a Father who throws parties for VIP sinners like you and me. At this point of the story, I am sure the Pharisees and teachers of the law who heard this were very aware of what was happening. In front of their very eyes was a stunning visual of what Jesus was talking about. Here was Jesus, at a party, eating and drinking with sinners in one big celebration of the lost and found, all welcomed by Jesus.

When I think of God's great love toward sinners like me, I cannot help but remember a story of a good friend of mine who embodied God's love in a powerful way.[4] He was speaking at a conference in Honolulu, and because Hawaii was in a different time zone from his home, he was having great difficulty sleeping at night. After a few sleepless nights, my friend gave up on trying to adjust his sleeping patterns and decided to visit a local all-night café a few blocks away from his hotel. Around three-thirty in the morning, while my friend was enjoying a coffee and donut, a group of female sex workers burst into the diner at the end of their busy night. They sat near my friend, sharing the only countertop in the small greasy spoon café. Then one of the women began to share with her friends that tomorrow would be her thirty-ninth birthday. Another of the women present sarcastically made fun of her, saying, "Well, good for you. What do you want from me? A party? Some nicely wrapped birthday gifts? Maybe a cake and candles and ice cream? Do you want me to sing 'Happy Birthday' for you? What do you want?"

In a sad, quiet voice the woman responded, "Why do you always have to be so mean? Why are you always putting me down? I'm just saying it's my birthday tomorrow, that's all. I'm not expecting anything. Why should I get anything anyway? I never had a birthday party in my life, so why should I get one now?"

The conversation continued for a little while longer before the sex workers left the diner. As the door closed behind them, my friend approached the cook who had served him his coffee and donut and inquired if these women were regular customers. He was told that they came to the diner around three-thirty every morning. My friend then asked the cook if he happened to know the name of the woman whose birthday was tomorrow, and was told her name was Agnes. So my friend shared with the cook an amazing idea he had. He said, "I heard Agnes say that it is her birthday tomorrow. How about we throw her a surprise birthday party? I'll pop over here tomorrow early, let's say at two-thirty, and I'll bring balloons, a banner, and a cake."

The cook thought this was a great idea and told my friend not to bother with the cake because he wanted to make Agnes a birthday cake himself.

The next morning my friend showed up an hour early to set up the banners and the balloons. There was a cake all ready, topped with candles and a "Happy Birthday, Agnes" design in icing. At three-thirty in the morning, the women walked into the diner as they always did and my friend, along with the cook and his wife, belted out a loud and boisterous, "Happy birthday, Agnes!" and they began to sing. Agnes was in shock. She was stunned as she looked around the diner, and then she began to cry. The cook encouraged Agnes to make a wish and blow out the candles. Once she finished, she was handed a knife and was asked to cut the cake so everyone could have a piece of her birthday cake in celebration of her life. Agnes just stood there in stunned silence. She couldn't keep her eyes off the cake. Then quietly she asked if she could take the cake home for a short while to show her mother before returning to enjoy the cake with her friends. Everybody present was dumbfounded. With their permission, off Agnes went, cake in hand, happy to have turned thirty-nine years old. This was the first time anyone hosted a birthday party for Agnes in her entire life. It was also her first birthday cake.

When she left, my friend asked everyone to form a circle and said, "Let's spend a few minutes praying for Agnes."

So my friend led prayer with a bunch of sex workers in a greasy spoon diner in Hawaii. When he was done, the cook leaned over to my friend and asked, "Hey, mister, you never told me you were a preacher. What kind of church do you belong to?"

My friend said, "I belong to a church that throws birthday parties for sex workers at three-thirty in the morning."

To which the cook responded, "No, you don't. There's no church like that. If there was, I would join that kind of church."

Here's the thing. We do belong to a church that throws parties for sex workers and all sinners like you and me. For if Jesus is the head of the church, then why wouldn't the church be on the forefront of throwing parties for lost sheep and prodigal children? After all, wasn't partying with sinners the modus operandi of Jesus? And is he not the head of the church?[5]

So how does God see us sinners? He welcomes us and eats with us, and even treats us sinners as VIPs while celebrating his love for each and every one of us.

QUESTIONS TO DISCUSS

Read Luke 15

1. Were there any "lightbulb" moments that struck you as being very important from this chapter? If yes, why were they important to you?

2. How do you think God sees you? Does God have a chart in which he ranks sinners in accordance with their sin, or does he see all of us as being the same?

3. From what you know about Jesus, how would you define scandalous, extraordinary grace?

4. What does it mean to be lost? Base your thoughts on what Jesus spoke about in his parables of the lost sheep, the lost coin, and the lost son. How have you been lost? How have you been found?

5. Do you think it is easier to judge than to love? What are some reasons people judge others? How can religion be used as a tool to energize judgmentalism?

6. Whom would you say you are most like in the parable of the prodigal—the younger son or the older son? Why do you feel this way?

7. Why would Jesus choose these descriptions for God—a shepherd seeking the one lost sheep, a woman searching for

her lost coin, and a loving father waiting for his lost son? Each of these parables ends with a massive party. What is the significance of celebration in the heart of God? What does this tell you about God?

8. What is one thing you will do this week in light of what you learned from this discussion?

PART TWO

HOW TO READ THE BIBLE TO FIND A GOD OF LOVE

*Every other portrait of God, from whatever source, is
subordinate to the revelation of God given us in Jesus
Christ. Jesus is the Word of God, the Logos of God, the
Logic of God in the form of human flesh. Christians are
to believe in the perfect, infallible, inerrant Word
of God—and his name is Jesus.*

—BRIAN ZAHND,
Sinners in the Hands of a Loving God

FIVE

The Confusion of Scripture

THE BIBLE IS A TERRIFYING BOOK, but I didn't realize how truly horrifying it was until I had children. As young parents, my wife and I wanted to read the Bible to our children as a bedtime ritual when they were old enough to understand the stories. Our plan was to put our children to sleep each night with a nice, gentle Bible story and a prayer. We thought this would be a great way to help our kids wind down from a busy, active day and enjoy a wonderful, peaceful sleep.

However, as time went on, we quickly realized that reading the Bible to children before they go to sleep may not be such a good idea after all. We soon discovered that many stories in the Bible were literal nightmares. As we looked down into our innocent children's eyes, we were shocked by the Bible. Oftentimes, the Bible sounds more like a Stephen King horror novel than a sweet children's storybook!

People and animals destroyed in a huge flood orchestrated by God. Firstborn sons killed by an angel of death. Egyptians drowned in the Red Sea. God commanding Israel to commit genocide by wiping out Canaanites, including men, women, children, and their animals. Ananias and Sapphira seemingly killed by God because of their disobedience. The future destruction of the world. Et cetera, et cetera. Not the most heartwarming stories to read to a child.

In light of these many R-rated stories, my wife and I decided to cherry-pick only the nice portions of the Bible to read to our children so that they would not be traumatized by what we read to them.

Let's face it. No matter how charming children's Bibles are, many of the stories in them are downright horrific. To make matters worse, history reveals how people have used the Bible to justify all sorts of evil. Take slavery, for example. During the years of American slavery, white enslavers bolstered their control of enslaved people by converting them to their brand of Christianity, which enforced this evil and oppressive system of bondage with a high dose of indoctrination through pro-slavery Bible verses.[1] The wicked cause of the slaveholders was affirmed by most church leaders of their day, who absurdly saw slavery as a powerful tool for evangelism. A Bible-believing bishop by the name of Stephen Elliott had this to say:

> For nearly a hundred years the English and American Churches have been striving to civilize and Christianize Western Africa, and with what result? Around Sierra Leone, and in the neighborhood of Cape Palmas, a few natives have been made Christians, and some nations have been partially civilized; but what a small number in

comparison with the thousands, nay, I may say millions, who have learned the way to Heaven and who have been made to know their Savior through the means of African slavery! At this very moment there are from three to four millions of Africans, educating for earth and for Heaven in the so vilified Southern States—learning the very best lessons for a semi-barbarous people—lessons of self-control, of obedience, of perseverance, of adaptation of means to ends; learning, above all, where their weakness lies, and how they may acquire strength for the battle of life. These considerations satisfy me with their condition, and assure me that it is the best relation they can, for the present, be made to occupy.[2]

In the eyes of the bishop, the slaveholder was a very effective evangelist!

The Bible has also been used to justify genocide.[3] In his book *Sinners in the Hands of a Loving God*, Brian Zahnd recounts the way that the Bible was used by colonists to justify wiping out Native American populations. He tells the story of the Pequot tribe, which was decimated by armed English colonists seeking to lay claim to Pequot land in the 1630s. Before the attack, and upon the request from his flock, the Reverend John Stone spent the night in prayer discerning what God wanted the colonists to do. The reverend reported back to the colonists that he had no moral qualms about initiating an unprovoked attack on the Pequot village. With the reverend's blessing, armed colonists killed between four and seven hundred innocent Indigenous people, most of whom were women and children. The commander of the colonists describes the massacre in biblical-like prose: "Thus was God seen in the Mount, crushing his proud enemies and the enemies of his people . . . burning them up in the fire of his wrath, and dunging the ground with their flesh: it was the Lord's doings and it is marvellous in our eyes."[4]

Upon hearing criticism from some of the colonists concerning the carnage, Captain John Underhill defended the butchery by appealing to the Bible, saying, "I would refer you to David's war. When a people is grown to such a height of blood and sin against God and man . . . sometimes the Scripture declareth women and children must perish with their parents. . . . We had sufficient light from the Word of God for our proceedings."[5]

Human extermination, justified by the Bible.

In case you think this kind of logic was something that only took place hundreds of years ago and would never be accepted by modern, more civilized people, I refer you to an interview with a contemporary popular Bible teacher who justifies genocide in the Bible, claiming, *"It's right for God to slaughter women and children anytime he pleases. God gives life and he takes life. Everybody who dies, dies because God wills that they die."* [6]

He goes on to say, "If I were to drop dead right now, or a suicide bomber downstairs were to blow this building up and I were blown into smithereens, God would have done me no wrong. He does no wrong to anybody when he takes their life, whether at two weeks or at age ninety-two. *God is not beholden to us at all. He doesn't owe us anything. Now add to that the fact we're all sinners and we deserve to die yesterday and go to hell yesterday, and the reality that we're even breathing today is sheer common grace from God."* [7]

To claim that God has the right to slaughter women and children (and men) anytime he pleases is extremely disturbing. Even worse is the statement that "God would have done me no wrong" by orchestrating a suicide bombing, as if such attacks were the will of God! Yet this strange belief that God has the right to kill anyone he pleases is a very common argument used to justify the Bible's account of a genocidal God. According to this belief, we—all of humanity—are filthy sinners, deserving the wrath of an offended God. Therefore, God has every right to kill anyone he wants. Any form of killing, including genocide, is justifiable if it is committed by God.

Another Bible teacher defends God's murderous ways, validating the killing of the Canaanite infants (see Deuteronomy 7:2; 20:16-17; Joshua 10:40; 11:14-15) by equating it to a salvific act! He writes, "If we believe, as I do, that God's grace is extended to those who die in infancy or as small children, the death of these children was actually their salvation. We are so wedded to an earthly, naturalistic perspective that we forget that those who die are happy to quit this earth for heaven's incomparable joy. Therefore, God does these children no wrong in taking their lives."[8]

It's hard to comprehend how teachers like this can be pro-life when it comes to abortion yet applaud the murder of infants in the Bible as a gracious act of God!

I understand where these earnest Bible teachers are coming from, since they are basing their views on the Bible. As with many other sincere Christians, their method of interpreting Scripture does not allow for divergent readings of violent texts. For them, the killing of women and children ceases to be a moral issue and becomes a Bible problem that must be solved. Although God's disturbing behavior might appear to be atrocious, it has to be justified. After all, if the Bible says it, then it must be true.

Yet the Bible seems to contradict itself in its view of violence. Did God not say, "Thou shalt not kill" (Exodus 20:13 KJV)? Isn't God one who is "good to all" and "has compassion on all he made" (Psalm 145:9)? Didn't Jesus say "anyone who has seen me has seen the Father" (John 14:9)? If this is the case, then how can we reconcile the Christlike God seen in Jesus with the sometimes violent genocidal God found in the Old Testament? Didn't Jesus command us to turn the other cheek instead of striking back (Matthew 5:38-39)? Did he not tell us to love our enemies and not kill them? Were we not told to pray for those who persecute us instead of destroying them (Matthew 5:43-44)? Are these commandments not also applicable to God during the Old Testament age? How can we reconcile these conflicting images of God in the Old Testament and God as seen in Jesus Christ?

Though the Bible can be used to justify terrible things, the opposite is true as well. Martin Luther King Jr. preached against racism by pointing to Scripture, even while many Christians in the Jim Crow South used the same Bible to support their racist views. In South Africa, some used the Bible to justify the dehumanizing system of apartheid, while at the same time local civil rights activists found strength in the Bible to fight apartheid. History shows us that those who fought for the rights of women to vote found their cause strengthened by Scripture, yet today many churches don't believe women have the right to be church leaders. In eighteenth- and nineteenth-century England, William Wilberforce was moved by Scripture to put an end to slavery, but today white nationalists use the Bible to support their despicable beliefs. Each cause can appeal to Scriptures to back up their argument, even if they are in complete disagreement with each other. How can this be? The answer is simple. It all hangs on how the Bible is read.

Whether the Bible is used for good or evil depends on how we read the Bible, and a big part of understanding what the

Bible really says depends on our view of God. This is why I spent the first few chapters of this book making a case for our need to have a loving image of God, because our view of God matters. If we believe we need to appease an angry God who separates himself from us because we are despicable sinners, then it's easy to agree with the vengeful verses we see in the Bible that justify violence. However, if we believe in a loving God who looks just like Jesus, we cannot accept an interpretation of the Bible that describes God in ways that are contrary to what Jesus is like. In these cases, we must learn to dig deeper into the Bible to understand what is really happening in the inspired text. This is exactly the position that the early church took for the first five hundred years of its existence. They believed that whenever we come across a portrayal of God that denigrates his loving character, we must pause and dig deeper to see if something else is happening in the story. They held to this belief because they were certain in their belief in a Christlike God as revealed to us in Jesus.

In the 1800s, self-emancipated abolitionist leader Frederick Douglass made a strong argument for the importance of reading the Bible based on an understanding of God as love. We see this in the way that he describes the huge chasm between the form of Christianity held by white enslaver Christians and the kind of Christianity that his fellow abolitionists lived out. The differences were based on the different interpretations of the Bible to which each side held. More specifically, these differences in interpretation stemmed from having a Christlike view of God as opposed to a non-Christlike view of God. Douglass states,

> Between the Christianity of this land and the Christianity of Christ, I recognize the widest possible difference—so

wide that to receive the one as good, pure, and holy, is of necessity to reject the other as bad, corrupt, and wicked. To be the friend of the one is of necessity to be the enemy of the other. I love the pure, peaceable, and impartial Christianity of Christ; I therefore hate the corrupt, slave-holding, women-whipping, cradle-plundering, partial and hypocritical Christianity of this land. Indeed, I can see no reason but the most deceitful one for calling the religion of this land Christianity.[9]

By sharing his insights into his context, Douglass touches on a method of how to read the Bible that aligns well with the understanding that Jesus came to reveal God as our *Abba* Daddy. Yet I am left with an important question—What do we do with the violent portrayals of God that are found in the Bible?

As a follower of Jesus, who told us to love our enemies, I am compelled to reject the idea of a God who chooses to kill his enemies. If Jesus is what God looks like in the flesh, then we have a Christlike God, and a God who looks like Jesus could never do the murderous things that we read about in the Bible. Yet by dismissing these negative portrayals of God, wouldn't I be guilty of not accepting the Bible as inspired by God? Even worse, would I be denying Jesus, who had such a high regard for the Scriptures, as is seen in the ways he often quoted the Hebrew Scriptures (what we now refer to as the Old Testament) as from God? On the other hand, if I believe that God condones genocide, slavery, and other detestable actions, wouldn't I also be guilty of denying the Bible as well? After all, how can Jesus and other New Testament authors declare that God is just like Jesus when God appears to have done horrible things that completely contradict the person, teachings, and character of Jesus? To add to our confusion, what do we do with the many Old

Testament Scriptures that portray a Christlike God of grace and love and that challenge other Old Testament Scriptures that speak of a graceless, spiteful, and violent God? What do we do with the Bible? Do we follow Jesus and his revelation of a God of love, accepting only Scriptures that portray God in this light? Or do we turn our back on Jesus' revelation of God to follow some biblical writers' views of God as vindicative?

One person who tried to get around this dilemma of opposing images of God was an early church leader named Marcion. Marcion acknowledged that the life and teachings of Jesus were completely incompatible with the violent behavior of God found in the Old Testament. This led Marcion to teach that there were two gods! For Marcion, there was a lower god of the Old Testament and a higher God of compassion as revealed by Jesus in the New Testament. Marcion was excommunicated in AD 144 for teaching his creative theory to explain the apparent discrepancies about God found in the Bible. As crazy as Marcion's heresy was, it goes to show how great the struggle to reconcile the conflicting views of God found in the Bible has been, an ongoing dilemma throughout church history.

For someone like me who believes in the divine inspiration of both the Old and New Testaments, Marcion's view of two competing gods is not an acceptable explanation. At the same time, I can't reconcile the completely opposite descriptions of a wrathful God and a loving, Christlike God. I found that I desperately needed to find a third option, and to do so I had to discover whether there is another way to read the Bible than the method I was taught. As I wrestled with how to interpret Scripture, I came to realize that the problem I was encountering with these two competing views of God was based on the fact that I thought the Bible could only be read as a "flat text." To read the Bible as a flat text means to take it literally without first examining the context, genre, and other voices of scriptural writers that can, at times, disagree with one another. By reading the Bible in this way I believed that the Bible was to be read like a moral cookbook or a rule book that taught me right from wrong. Like many others, I had believed that God dictated every word of the Bible through the mind of an inspired writer who acted more like a robot than a human being. In this view, the Bible is seen as a divine instruction manual that coldly dispenses truths that we must live up to or is reduced to a textbook to be read as literally as possible. But what if I was wrong? What if the Bible is more than a moral cookbook? What if it is deeper and more impactful than the limitations of a flat text?

When I think of the limitations of reading the Bible as a flat text, I liken it to my experiences with backpacking trips I led for urban youth. I loved those trips, as they were a great time to get out of the city for a few days, allowing me the opportunity to challenge city youth to be pushed beyond their self-made limitations. My goal was to help these youths grow in their personal confidence and self-awareness before returning home. Each year I would take fifteen youth to hike into the wilds with our own food, camping supplies, pup tents, and a map of the trail we were to follow. After doing a few of these camping trips, I quickly learned that nature's most breathtaking views and the most exciting experiences of hiking took place off the safely groomed path. Staying on the marked trail was good, but following the side trails that took us off the beaten path to camp in the wilds was exhilarating, and clearly the most life-transforming experience for our crew.

We limit the Bible's impact when we stick to the simple, straight-and-narrow, flat-text hiking trail of the Scriptures. By limiting our Bible reading to the safe, well-groomed, flat-text trails, we are prevented from discovering the many side paths that God wants us to explore that come along the way. Strict adherence to a literal reading allows us to experience some of God. However, it prevents us from noticing deeper and more incredible views of God that are experienced only when we go off-trail. Oftentimes, the true adventure of encountering God takes place outside the flat text when we hike through hidden mountain pathways and cascading valleys to the streams of true living water.

By reading the Bible as a flat text, we cannot help but run into the problems of conflicting images of God as a God of wrath or as a God who looks like Jesus. This is because a flat-text reading of the Bible is often limited to the most easily apparent meaning of the words that are written on the page, words that at times can actually contradict each other.

But for these words to have deeper significance and clearer meaning, they need to be read along other pathways that veer off the main trail. Taking the hike off-trail allows us to feel a fresh wind of energy that draws us on an adventurous journey with the Holy Spirit as we take a slow climb from one level of inspiration to a higher and more complete level of divine truth and reality. This side trail leads to more of God and deeper revelation. Experiencing this kind of biblical inspiration cannot come about through a flat-text reading of Scripture. We must go deeper by being willing to deviate from the limitations of the flat-text trail.

If the Bible is to be read only as a flat text, we have no other option than to accept the impossibility of divergent views of God and to believe in a loving, hateful, forgiving, angry, healing, genocidal maniac who commands his followers to kill their enemies even though he said, "Thou shall not kill." Of course, this does not make any sense at all. Instead, when we come across an image of God that opposes God's character as a God of love, we need to be willing to get off the simple flat-text hiking trail, no matter how uncomfortable it may make us feel, and take a side trail. This is because, in these instances, the flat-text, instruction-manual way of reading the Bible no longer works. It is not complete enough. Yet all is not lost. The simple pathway of reading the Bible as a flat text is good if we recognize that it leads us onto side paths into the depth of the forest. This is where the God of the inspired words wants us to go. When this happens, there are a few choices we can make.

The first and best choice is to be adventurous readers who are willing to leave the flat-text trail to embrace the challenge ahead. We can choose to be open to following the Spirit's lead to take us along the rock-strewn side paths deeper into the wilderness. Sadly, most Bible readers are too afraid to be Spirit-led, pioneering hikers. They just give up on the Bible when they do not like where it has taken them, rejecting the flat-text reading, and thus the entire Bible, controlled by a fear to go deeper into the backwoods. Other readers are stubborn, choosing safety over adventure to continue following the same old flat-text trail no matter what. They worry about those left behind who have given up on the Bible and tend to get angry with the adventurers who willingly take on the challenge to go deeper than where the flat-text trail has led them. Most of those staying on the flat-text path become fixated on the old trail and make an idol of it, failing to realize that the purpose of the trail is to lead them deeper into God. These trail worshipers become engrossed in bibliolatry, in which the Bible is placed on the same level as the Holy Trinity.

The scary thing about bibliolatry is that it allows people to claim that their interpretation of Scripture is the full, authoritative Word of God. At the same time, other Biblicists who disagree with them can also claim full biblical authority for their own contrasting view. When this happens, the flat-text trail quickly becomes a dangerous path of division. How many times have you heard someone defend their point of view as being biblical or shout down someone else's beliefs as being unbiblical? As a result, neither will listen to the other person's view, because bibliolatry allows each to be their own private authority for what they choose to read into the flat text. This allows for the potential to approve of terrible actions such as genocide, slavery, patriarchy, unjust political actions, and violence against whomever we label as our enemies to be justified through the Bible. It's also why we have well over 33,830 different denominations in Christianity, as people choose different ways to read the flat text![10]

One of the most glaring examples of the way that a flat-text view of the Bible doesn't work is evidenced in the famous 1925 court case known as the Scopes trial. Substitute teacher John T. Scopes was accused of breaking state law by teaching evolution in the classroom. Christians, enraged by Scopes's actions, argued against evolution by using Scriptures as their authority. These Christians had a very high view of Scripture as the Word of God. But while many of these defenders of the Bible fought against evolution being taught in their schools, many were also supporters of a system of racial oppression that included lynching African Americans and burning their homes. This is what can happen when people bring their presuppositions to a flat text for theological justification. They can interpret the Bible as opposing a belief in evolution because they see it as undercutting the value of humans as being created in God's image, yet at the same time they can use the Bible to justify the active brutalization of people who are also created in God's image.

As we end this chapter, I must ask, Which pathway are you on? Are you feeling burdened and confused on the narrow flat-text trail? Have you given up completely on your faith because the flat-text trail has led you to a place you no longer want to be? Or have you been able to see the ways that the flat-text trail you once journeyed has led to other pathways that allow you to discover a deeper experience of God?

As I struggled with biblical inspiration and the opposing views of God as seen in Scripture, it became quite obvious to me that a flat view of the Bible does not work. Surely, there had to be another way of reading the Bible. So I searched for a way I could be faithful both to the Scriptures and to Jesus' portrayal of a loving God found in the Bible. This led me to study church history, ancient Jewish culture, and Jesus' and Paul's methods of understanding Scripture to see how they made sense of all of this. While going through this process, I was pleasantly surprised by what I found.

QUESTIONS TO DISCUSS

Read Psalm 119:97-112

1. Were there any "lightbulb" moments that struck you as being very important from this chapter? If yes, why were they important to you?

2. What are some stories or verses you don't like in the Bible? Why don't you like them?

3. How can people use Scripture to justify evil? Have you seen this happen in the past?

4. How do you deal with contradictory depictions of an angry God versus a Christlike God?

5. Frederick Douglass opposed slavery in part on the grounds of what he called the "Christianity of Christ." What qualities are present in a Christianity of Christ? How does following a Christianity of Christ equip us to deal with passages that depict God as un-Christlike?

6. Marcion dealt with the opposing views of God by espousing a heresy that depicted two gods—a lower, angry god of the Old Testament and another, higher god, found in Jesus. Without being a Marcionite, what are some ways you deal with the contradictory views of God or verses you don't like from the Bible? How do others deal with these challenges?

7. How do you read the Bible? Do you stick to a flat-text reading, or do you incorporate other methods in your reading?

8. What is one thing you will do this week in light of what you learned from this discussion?

SIX

How to Read the Bible

TO BE FAITHFUL to the Bible means we must first be faithful to its author. Since God is the creative mind behind the Bible, we must humbly admit that God also has poetic license over how the Bible was written. As the author, God also has every right to determine how his book should be read. This leads to the question, How does God want the Bible to be read? As mentioned earlier, many would answer this question by affirming a flat-text reading. But is this the correct answer? What if God desires that we read his book differently? Since the Bible is "God-breathed " (2 Timothy 3:16), we must acknowledge that it is much greater, more impactful, vastly deeper, and more life transforming than any book ever written in the history of humankind.

Great works of literature tend to be ageless. They speak messages to the soul that transcend the pages of a book. Since this is the case with especially gifted authors, we can only expect that anything written by God would exceed any human literary masterpiece. How could we think otherwise? When I think about how the Bible should be read, I'd like to take us back to the last chapter when I shared a story of taking urban youth to experience the great outdoors. I will never forget one particular trip in which we got lost on our hike back after a weekend of camping. As we took to the trail for our way back home, I noticed that the bright plastic trail markers that mark the hiking trail were no longer tied to the tree branches. I thought this was strange, since we had followed them on our hike in just a few days earlier. Fortunately for us, there was only one trail out, so we began our trek back to the parking lot without needing the bright orange signs. This worked well until we came across a fork in the trail. Without trail markers, I didn't know if we should take the right trail fork or the left. In a state of mild confusion, and with a degree of fear at the possibility of being lost in the woods with a group of urban youth, I asked our group to help me look for the trail markers to guide us home. After a short time of looking for the bright plastic markers, one of the youths exclaimed, "Oh, are these what you are looking for?"

As he waved the precious bright orange trail markers in his hands, I couldn't believe what I saw. He explained that on the hike in he had taken the markers off the branches as souvenirs, not realizing what they were for. Without these markers to guide us, we were now forced to enter a real adventure. We were forced to come together as a team, to read the trail map, follow a compass, and pray for guidance. Together, energized by plenty of animated discussion, we were able to navigate our way back to the parking lot. We were exhausted, but better off from enjoying the challenge as we learned to be dependent on God and one another. Looking back on this adrenaline-filled adventure, I can see how hiking off-trail was a transformative experience as we discovered more about who we were as individuals and as a group.

Hiking is a great metaphor for how to read Scripture. To read the Bible, we need to first follow the clear markers found along the flat-text trail. This is important, and I am thankful for this simple and faithful way of reading Scripture. However, in time, you quickly realize that these markers often guide you to a confusing fork in the path. This fork occurs when something you read that is attributed to God does not line up to the image of God as seen in Jesus. When this happens, it is time to get off the well-trodden flat-text trail and veer off onto an exciting side trail. This is what good Bible readers do. They are willing to experience a degree of discomfort as they navigate the many twists and turns found on the Bible's pages. On this side path, you will find yourself creeping along steep climbs and dangerous drops, walking in dry deserts, struggling through rushing rivers, stepping in lush fields, and stumbling along thorny ground. Yet it is here, on this journey, that you will experience God speaking to you through the Bible. This is why it is important not to remain stuck on the tedious flat-text trail, where you experience only part of the terrain. An adventurous journey with God awaits beyond the well-marked path.[1]

Too many Bible readers are not willing to honestly wrestle with the Scriptures. They don't like putting on their hiking boots to go on a tough hike, preferring the easy, well-maintained beginner's trails instead. If they read the Bible at all, they settle on a simple flat reading, and when they come across something that really challenges them or offends their sensibilities, they gloss over it or ignore it completely. For them, the Bible can easily become a boring hike. With no surprises or exciting challenges to explore, they might give up hiking because of boredom. Other Bible readers choose to cherry-pick verses they like and blissfully ignore the verses they dislike. Many will not go deep with their questions and rely instead on outside sources, such as a pastor, to provide them with rote answers. This is like asking someone to describe an exciting hiking trail to you, but never experiencing that trail by hiking it yourself. This is not the way to read the Bible.

Do you want to hike the fullness of the Bible? Are you ready to take an awesome trek in the Scriptures? If your answer is yes, then grab your hiking boots and let's get ready to go! But before we head out, it is important to understand a few things as we get ready to embark on the adventure of a lifetime.

To read the Bible well, we must take the following steps.

STEP 1: **BE MENTALLY PREPARED FOR THE HIKE AHEAD**

The first thing good Bible hikers know is that what they are about to embark on is full of mystery. They understand that the Bible was written as a book of wisdom, and as such, it will not always provide simple answers or set rules for the hike. God wants to use the Bible, as a book of wisdom, to pull you out of your mundane way of thinking by making you uncomfortable in areas of your life where you need to be challenged. The Holy Spirit invites you to wrestle with the Bible's truths and argue with its content, for it is in this struggle with Scripture that you grow spiritually. Expect to be surprised and challenged. Be open and willing to embrace the struggles along the way. As Peter Enns states so well, "The Bible, it seems to me, was never intended to work as a step-by-step instructional manual. Rather, it presents us with an invitation to explore. Or better, the Bible, simply by being an ancient, ambiguous, and diverse self, blocks us from the simple path of seeking from it clear answers and rather herds us toward a more subtle, interesting, and above all sacred quest."[2]

If you find that your reading of the Bible doesn't stretch or challenge you, or if it always makes you feel safe and comfortable, then you are probably not reading the Bible properly. Reading the Bible should not be safe and easy. God wants to stretch you, break you, and rebuild you as you journey through this strenuous path to divine wisdom. Never forget this. As a book of wisdom, the Bible is written in a way that will cause a chain reaction in your mind and soul. What you read can give you a feeling of great peace or leave you feeling very upset. This is all part of great Bible hiking, because the Bible, as a wisdom book, is not to be read as a simple rule book to placate or control you. The Bible is far bigger and better than that! God intends for it to challenge your way of thinking so it can change your way of living.

That the Bible is seen as a book of wisdom is clearly depicted in 2 Timothy 3, where we read, "But as for you, *continue in what you have learned* and have *become convinced of,* because you know those from whom *you learned it,* and how from infancy you have known the Holy Scriptures, which are *able to make you wise* for salvation through faith in Christ Jesus. All Scripture is God-breathed and is *useful for teaching, rebuking, correcting and training* in righteousness, so that the servant of God may be thoroughly equipped for every good work" (vv. 14-17).[3]

Notice the italicized words in the text above that show how one grows in wisdom. These words reveal to us that a proper reading of Scripture is an ongoing, humble process of wrestling with its content. Timothy had "become convinced," which suggests a progression of insight, not a simple acceptance. Timothy also "learned it" from others, which meant that Timothy was a humble apprentice with a teachable heart. We also see that

Timothy was very active in this learning process. The ancient Hebraic way of teaching Scripture involved what is called sacred argument or debate, as opposed to passively accepting what is taught. In this way Timothy had to wrestle with Scripture by undergoing times of rebuking, correcting, and training as part of his learning process. All of these dynamic verbs suggest an interactive and challenging way to understand Scripture, as opposed to the dry and passive ways that North Americans are often taught the Bible.

We would be wise to learn from this trail master. Timothy understood how to hike the Bible. His model is a powerful motivator for us to embrace the Bible as a book of wisdom that is "able to make you wise for salvation through faith in Christ Jesus" (v. 15).

STEP 2: **START THE HIKE ON THE MARKED TRAIL OF THE FLAT TEXT**

With the right mindset, you are now ready to begin your hike. It is here that you begin your hike by reading the Bible as a flat text, noticing the most apparent and literal meaning of the words. While you do this, you may want to add a few different Bible translations into the mix to shine different angles of light along the pathway. Remember that this is just the beginning of your journey that will lead you to the wild and inspired side trails awaiting you further along the way.

STEP 3: **PAUSE ON THE HIKE WHEN YOU FACE QUESTIONS FROM YOUR READING**

As you enjoy the beauty of the flat-text trail, you will eventually stumble upon something you read that makes you question the goodness of God. When this happens, do not ignore or discount any questions or doubts that might arise from your reading, because they provide vital pathways that the Holy Spirit wants us to travel. This is where you need to stop and ponder what you are reading. The Spirit has guided you to this point of the trail and wants you to discover a side path, trusting the Holy Spirit for guidance each step of the way. The Bible is a wonderful yet mysterious book. If you are to be influenced by its truths, more is needed than human reasoning alone. The Spirit has been given to you as your guide, comforter, and counselor.[4]

STEP 4: **USE YOUR HIKING TOOLS**

At this point in your hike, it is helpful to whip out a hiking map to help guide you along the rugged side trail. Maps are created by topographers, experts who have charted the area and know the natural terrain, providing a helpful tool for backwoods hikers. In our case, the hiking maps we use are Bible encyclopedias, dictionaries, commentaries, and more literal translations of the words we are reading. This might sound complicated or expensive, but you can find all of these tools for free online.[5] When you come to know the deeper meanings of the words you are reading, and understand the culture and context in which the words were written, this knowledge will shine more light to direct you on your trail.

STEP 5: **JOURNEY THE NEW PATH TOGETHER WITH HIKING BUDDIES**

By stepping onto the side path, you are now enabled to take the exciting journey toward wisdom, following where your questions have led you. Trust in the Holy Spirit to show you the way. At the same time, it is beneficial to have hiking buddies join you on the trail. Though we can get a lot out of personal

Bible reading, it is important to recognize that the Bible is not meant to be read alone and is best read in community with others who can help shine light on the Scriptures through shared insights and experiences, and even through all-out debate. As a book of wisdom, the Bible was built for debate! All one has to do is read the life of Jesus in the Gospels, and you will see how much Jesus debated Scripture. It was both an effective teaching method and a way to learn wisdom.

In fact, if you were to go to Jerusalem today and visit a Jewish *yeshiva* (seminary), you would notice that the way Scripture is taught and learned is completely different from the way learning takes place in Western Christian seminaries. In a yeshiva, there are fewer lectures and more debate. You would see and hear students prodding each other by arguing and challenging one another regarding their interpretations of Scripture, with the goal of coming to an understanding of what is being read. All of this is done within an atmosphere of civility.[6] In fact, holy debate is such a prime importance for these students that they are expected to be part of a Jewish *haverim*, a group of people who study the Bible together to help each other master the text.[7] We see Jesus modeling this methodology of discipleship with his followers, who formed a haverim, a community of disciples who lived and learned together, and were often seen asking questions or arguing over the teachings of Jesus with one another.

Authors Ann Spangler and Lois Tverberg describe what a good haverim buddy looks like when they write,

> A *haver* is a fellow disciple who earnestly desires to grapple with others over issues of faith—someone who wants to delve into God's Word, to be challenged and refined.

A *haver* is like a spiritual "jogging partner"—someone for whom you'll crawl out of bed on a rainy morning, putting on your running shoes instead of hitting the snooze button. Once you're up and running together, your pace is a little faster, you keep going a little longer. You are pushed intellectually and spiritually. If we really want to mature in faith and as disciples, we need to develop relationships that force us to grow, by getting ourselves some *haverim*.[8]

In our case, a haverim could also be pictured as a group of fellow hikers who journey the trail with one another, pushing each other to keep moving forward and deeper along the path when the going gets tough. Needless to say—we all need a haverim!

Debate is of prime importance to our Jewish friends, as they believe they cannot have a religious life without holy arguing. They describe this as a sacred art form known as "arguing for the sake of heaven."[9] For them, debating to learn the truth of Scripture is a form of worship, right alongside prayer, showing that they truly are faithful and devoted to God. Holy arguing is a sacred duty and a holy delight. Their understanding is that the sacred Scriptures are so precious that they are worth fighting over in order to understand them.

Unlike our Jewish brothers and sisters, many Christians shy away from questioning the Bible. This is because belief in a flat reading tends to quash any form of holy debate. Rather than allowing for sacred arguments to take place as a humble way to read the Bible, flat-text churches tend to ostracize those who do not agree with them. Haverims cannot take place in these types of churches, as they prefer to stay within their own protective yet boring bubble consisting of those who see everything the same way. Without acknowledging the Bible as a book of wisdom from God that needs to be wrestled with, there is no hope of having a sacred argument about its meaning. A "the Bible said it, I believe it, that settles it" view of Scripture not only creates enemies of those whom we might not agree with but also closes the door on listening and learning through the space of humble debate. This is very different from the way Jesus and Jewish culture read Scripture. "The Torah started the discussion. For many in our world, the Bible ends the discussion. Someone stands up and reads from the Bible and then tells the gathered masses what it means and what is right and how it should be interpreted and then the service is over and everybody leaves. But in the first-century world of Jesus, the Torah and the Prophets and the wisdom writings were the start of the discussion."[10]

For Jews, sacred arguing was the simple result of accepting the rabbinical tradition that describes the Bible as having seventy faces or as being like a diamond reflecting different angles of light. They saw the Scriptures as not limited to only one face but having many faces and angles that mirror the depths of insights to be discovered and that lead to wisdom. The Bible is big and wonderful and lively. Scripture is not limited to a single flat view that ends all arguments; rather, it possesses many meanings, insights, and applications. This is why you often hear people exclaim, "I have read that verse countless times, and each time I read it, I learn something new." Jesus was Jewish. He embraced and worshiped the Father through sacred argument. Perhaps as followers of Jesus, we too should learn the humble art of holy argument from him instead of engaging in divisive Bible-thumping.

Newness in understanding. Seeing different truths. Developing new perceptions and applications. Gaining countless insights. All of these experiences are found in your Bible, and each verse teems with transformative life as God breathes different meanings into what you read. The Bible truly has seventy faces, and because of this, we study, think about, wrestle with, and yes, even argue about each possible face. We challenge what we see, look at it from different angles, turn it over again and again to see its many possibilities. This is also why it is important to be involved in a haverim, because more can be seen through the eyes of many than through the vision of one. Invite others to join you on the hike through the Bible, and include those hikers who have come before us. As you hold sacred arguments with one another in your haverim, feel free to include the thoughts of hiking legends like the early church fathers and theologians from the past, and even sprinkle in some modern Christian thinkers to allow them a voice in the holy argument. Hiking the Bible with others and practicing the art of sacred argument is vital for gaining wisdom from the trails that the Scriptures will take you on.

DON'T FORGET YOUR BINOCULARS!

There is one final and most important thing you need to take with you throughout the entire hike. You need to become familiar with and utilize a Jesus lens. A Jesus lens is like a great pair of binoculars that will help you navigate the trail well. It allows you to see from the beginning to the very end of the trail and clarifies the right direction. It is vital to make sure that every passage of Scripture and each verse of the Bible passes through this Jesus lens if we are to understand it properly. In fact, holding a Jesus lens to Scripture will often cause you to question what you are reading and send you off on another exciting adventure down a side pathway where you will discover new truths.

In Luke 24:13-35, we see a great example of how important it is to have a Jesus lens when reading Scripture. This passage also gives us a terrific example of how to read the Bible, as it contains the many steps we mentioned in this chapter. In this story, two followers of Jesus were hiking together from Jerusalem to a village called Emmaus. As they began their walk, they were in deep conversation concerning the crucifixion of their rabbi, Jesus, and struggling with some confusing reports they had recently heard. Apparently, a rumor was making the rounds that his body was missing. "As they talked and discussed these things with each other, Jesus himself came up and walked along with them; but they were kept from recognizing him" (vv. 15-16).

Some people believe that Cleopas and his friend were kept from recognizing Jesus because his resurrected body made him look different. Others believe that the psychological grief that Cleopas and his friend were enduring blinded them from recognizing that Christ was in their presence. Or maybe God kept them from recognizing that Jesus was with them because God wanted to show them what the Scriptures had to say about Jesus. Possibly, it was a combination of some or all the above factors.

When Jesus joined them, he asked, "What are you discussing together as you walk along?" (v. 17).

Shocked to hear such a question, Cleopas responded, "Are you the only one visiting Jerusalem who does not know the things that have happened there in these days?" (v. 18).

Obviously, Jesus knew what had happened, as he was the central character in this horrific event. So this makes Jesus' response to Cleopas's question surprising. Jesus asked, "What things?" (v. 19).

Jesus responded to Cleopas's question with a question of his own. This is an example of a wise teacher using questions to guide people to a reality of which they might not be aware. By asking this important question, Jesus set the stage for Cleopas and his friend to come to understand why Jesus came, lived, died, and rose again.

As Cleopas and his friend spent hours hiking together with the unidentified Jesus, time must have flown by as they participated in their own haverim. I can picture them walking that dusty trail from Jerusalem to Emmaus asking questions, challenging each other's ideas, and arguing with one another. This is something with which they would have been very comfortable, since it is how people of their culture gained wisdom. During their haverim conversation, we read, "And beginning with Moses and all the Prophets, [Jesus] explained to them what was said in all the Scriptures concerning himself" (v. 27).

Here we see Christ himself using his Jesus lens to shine truth on the Scriptures and help clarify what they said about him. Jesus took Cleopas and his friend on a wild side path, far away from what they read in the flat text, to be able to understand what the Bible was really saying.

Eventually, they reached Emmaus, where during dinner, the eyes of Cleopas and his friend were opened to recognize that their new friend who had been with them was Jesus.

When they realized this, they asked, "Were not our hearts burning within us while he talked with us on the road and opened the Scriptures to us?" (v. 32).

This is what happens when the Scriptures make an impact on your soul.

Once Cleopas and his friend recognized Jesus was with them, we read that Jesus disappeared from their presence. The lesson had been taught and it was time for the teacher to move on. For Cleopas and his friend, spending time in a haverim with the resurrected Jesus shining light into the Scriptures must have been thrilling. In fact, this experience was so amazing that we read that they immediately went all the way back to Jerusalem to inform the eleven disciples that Jesus was indeed risen.

Imagine if you were on that hike with Jesus, Cleopas, and his friend. How incredible it would have been to listen and discuss Scripture with Jesus. Yet Jesus is risen, and because of this reality, the resurrected Jesus still guides us to truth when we read the Bible through a Jesus lens, just as Jesus did with Cleopas and his friend.

Get ready to grab your hiking boots and backpack, get familiar with tools you need, grab some hiking buddies, and get prepared to let Jesus guide you as you hike the Bible. But before you do all of this, let's take a look at the unique ways Jesus and the apostle Paul understood the Bible so we can delve deeper, learning more hiking tips from these master hikers.

QUESTIONS TO DISCUSS

Read Luke 24:13-35

1. Were there any "lightbulb" moments that struck you as being very important from this chapter? If yes, why were they important to you?

2. What does it mean to you to describe the Bible as a divine book of wisdom?

3. Why do you think people struggle with the concept of questioning the Bible? Why do you think people in Jesus' culture, including Jesus himself, had no problem with questioning Scripture?

4. In what ways can sacred arguments be holy acts of worship? What would you envision as the ground rules to be followed to have constructive sacred debates?

5. How could participating in a haverim be important in your context? How do you see a haverim mentality as being beneficial to the church at large? What steps do you think would need to take place to create a haverim?

6. How do you see a Jesus lens working when reading Scripture?

7. What is one thing you will do this week in light of what you learned from this discussion?

SEVEN

How Jesus and Paul Read Scripture

IF YOU HAVE EVER BEEN to an amusement park or county fair, you have undoubtedly come across the carnival game known as the shell game. In this game, the contestant is presented with three identical upside-down cups, one of which holds a small ball. The game begins when the cups are moved and mixed on a table at varying speeds. The challenge is to keep track of which cup has the hidden ball inside it. This isn't as easy as you might think, since the game master is very good with sleight of hand. After a minute or so of the constant swirl of moving cups, the choice must be made to decide which cup contains the ball underneath it.

Many people today have been playing a shell game with Jesus. It is as if we have various images of Jesus swirling around us, and our challenge is to spot which one is the real Jesus.

You might have seen the popular T-shirt that has a smiling and winking Jesus, with his thumbs up, that states, "Jesus is my homeboy." This is a good example of a fake image of Jesus that is part of the religious shell game. He's our buddy Jesus who exists to always make us happy, blesses us nonstop, and makes us feel good. He's the Jesus who always brings the beer to the party! He doesn't demand much from us, because he's our homeboy, with his thumbs up, smiling at us no matter what we think, do, or say. But he's a false cup Jesus.

A second fake image of Jesus that is a big part of the religious shell game that many have constructed in their minds is the mirror Jesus. He's the Jesus that looks just like us, the Jesus we create to justify our own behavior and actions. This Jesus should not surprise us, because sociologists have discovered that in every culture people tend to create a God just like them.

We have created this Jesus to look and act just like us. For me, this Jesus is a white Irish Canadian who loves hockey and a good plate of greasy chicken wings, and who believes exactly what I believe. For some Americans, their Jesus might look like a hard-nosed Republican who wants to put America first. Or maybe their Jesus appears more like a soft Democrat who wants to increase taxes to share the wealth. Either way, we all seem to have this tendency toward believing in a Jesus that looks just like us. We would rather have a Jesus who follows us than for us to follow him.

One of the best examples of this mirror Jesus is found in the city of Colorado Springs, the home of the U.S. Air Force Academy. Located on their property is a place of worship that is shaped in the form of fighter jets. Inside the chapel, there is a large cross hanging from the ceiling made to look like a sword. How ironic and difficult it must be to worship the Prince of Peace inside a chapel that looks like a weapon of war containing a cross-like sword.[1]

The point is that we all have the tendency to tame Jesus so we can have divine approval for what we want and stand for. They are false cup Jesuses in a cheap religious game of shell cup worship.

There is a phrase to describe this kind of faith—easy believism. Easy believism might be the most popular form of Christianity there is today, as it provides a lot of wiggle room to justify anything you want it to.

This leaves us with the third Jesus. The third Jesus is the real Jesus, but he is the "hard to believe Jesus." This isn't because we doubt his existence. No, this Jesus exists. The problem is that it's hard to believe in what this Jesus says because his teachings are in complete opposition to the false Jesuses that we prefer. Truth be told, it is hard to deal with this third Jesus, who commands us to love our enemies. That Jesus is hard to believe in, isn't he? What about this third Jesus who tells me to pray for those who do me harm? It's tough to believe in him. What about this third Jesus who tells me to sacrificially give to the poor? Man, he's tough to believe in, right? What do I do about this third Jesus who tells me to turn the other cheek and walk the extra mile, to bless those who hate me?

As one journalist describes so well,

Jesus unambiguously preached mercy and forgiveness. These are supposed to be cardinal virtues of the Christian faith. And yet Evangelicals are the most supportive of the death penalty, draconian sentencing, punitive punishment over rehabilitation, and the governmental use of torture. Jesus exhorted humans to be loving, peaceful, and non-violent. And yet Evangelicals are the group of Americans most supportive of easy-access weaponry, little-to-no regulation of handgun and semi-automatic gun ownership, not to mention the violent military invasion of various countries around the world. . . . Evangelicals are the most supportive of corporate greed and capitalistic excess, and they are the most opposed to institutional help for the nation's poor— especially poor children. . . . In short, Evangelicals are that segment of America which is the most pro-militaristic, pro-gun, and pro-corporate, while simultaneously claiming to be most ardent lovers of the Prince of Peace.[2]

Do you see why this real Jesus has been replaced by a fake Jesus? Though it is true that the real Jesus is a blessing and saving Jesus, he also tells us to love our enemies, turn the other cheek, do good to those who hurt us, and be willing to suffer by taking up our cross to follow him. Now those are hard words to swallow.

Comedian and self-acclaimed atheist Bill Maher might know the real Jesus better than many Christians do. He satirically describes the Jesus shell game taking place all around us:

If you're a Christian that supports killing your enemy and torture, you have to come up with a new name for yourself. . . . "Capping the enemy" is not exactly what Jesus would do. For almost two thousand years, Christians have been lawyering the Bible to try to figure out how "Love thy neighbour" can mean "Hate thy neighbour." . . .

Martin Luther King Jr. gets to call himself a Christian, because he actually practiced loving his enemies. And Gandhi was so [expletive] Christian, he was a Hindu. But if you're endorsing revenge, torture or war . . . you cannot say you're a follower of the guy who explicitly said, "Love your enemy" and "Do good to those who hate you." . . .

And not to put too fine a point on it, but nonviolence was kind of Jesus' trademark—kind of his big thing. To not follow that part of it is like joining Greenpeace and hating whales. There's interpreting, and then there's just ignoring. It's just ignoring if you're for torture—as are more Evangelical Christians than any other religion. You're supposed to look at that figure of Christ on the Cross and think, "how could a man suffer like that and forgive?" . . .

I'm a non-Christian. *Just like most Christians.*

If you ignore every single thing Jesus commanded you to do, you're not a Christian—you're just auditing. You're not Christ's followers, you're just fans. And if you believe the earth was given to you to kick [a**] on while gloating, you're not really a Christian—you're a Texan.[3]

One of the greatest fallback plans many of us have to silence the real Jesus is to appeal to the Old Testament. It's the greatest trick that can be used to put the real Jesus in his place. How better to stand up to Jesus and question his teachings of peace than to use violent passages we find in the Old Testament? Yet this puts us in a real dilemma. It forces us to ask the following questions:

How are we to reconcile the God revealed in Christ, who chose to die for his enemies rather than crush them, with the many Old Testament portraits of Yahweh violently smiting his enemies? How are we to reconcile the God revealed in Christ, who made swearing off violence a precondition for being considered a "a child of your father in heaven" (Matt 5:45), with the portraits of Yahweh commanding his followers to slaughter every man, woman, child, and animal in certain regions of Canaan (Deut 7:2; 20:16-20)? How are we to reconcile the God revealed in Christ, who with his dying breath prayed for the forgiveness of his tormentors (Luke 22:34) and who taught the disciples to forgive "seven times seventy" (Matt 18:21-22) with the Old Testament portraits of God threatening a curse on anyone who extended mercy toward enemies (Jer 48:10; cf. Deut 7:2, 16; 13:8; 19:13)? And how can we possibly reconcile the God revealed in Christ, who professed profound love for children, promising blessings on all who treated them well and pronouncing warnings for all who might harm them (Luke 18:15-17; Matt 10:42; 18:6-14), with the [Old Testament] portrait of God bringing judgement on his people by having parents cannibalize their own children (Lev 26:28-29; Jer 19:7, 9; Lam 2:20; Ezek 5:9-10)?[4]

How do we deal with these texts in the Bible that portray God to be the opposite of Jesus?

In his seminal two-volume set entitled *The Crucifixion of the Warrior God*, Greg Boyd has written extensively on making sense of violent portrayals of God. In volume 2, Boyd shares a great illustration to help us understand how to hike the biblical side trails we come across when we read about an easily angered God who smites others. Boyd describes his wife as the most generous and loving person he has ever known, and then proceeds to build an imaginative story to illustrate his point. In his story, he imagines inadvertently witnessing his loving, kind, and tenderhearted wife attacking a poor, weak, homeless beggar on the streets. In shock, he watches her scream and rage at the old man, slapping him in his face and kicking him out of his wheelchair. Since her behavior is so unlike the woman he knows so well, he is forced to assume that something else has to be happening behind the scenes. The outrageous behavior of his wife is so out of character with whom he knows her to be that her behavior must mean that something is going on beyond the obvious. Perhaps this is not an old man, but a sex offender using a disguise to lure unsuspecting people to him so he can hurt them, and Boyd's wife is subduing him to stop his behavior? Or maybe there is a hidden camera nearby and his wife is part of a humorous plot, using actors, to surprise her husband? In either case, something has to be happening behind the scenes that Boyd is unaware of, since there is no way his compassionate wife would act so out of character.[5]

Boyd uses this illustration to explain that when we look at passages of Scripture where God seems to act out of character when compared to Christ, or when God appears to act in a coldhearted, violent, and vengeful manner, we have to acknowledge that something else must be happening behind the scenes of these verses. This is because there is no way that a Christlike God would behave in such an un-Christlike manner.

So where do we go from here?

Brian Zahnd provides helpful guidance when it comes to understanding violent portrayals of God. He states that there really are only three options before us:

1. We can question the morality of God. Perhaps God is, at times, monstrous?

2. We can question the immutability of God. Maybe God does change over time?

3. We can question how we read Scripture. Could it be that we need to learn how to read the Bible in a different way?[6]

The first two options are off the table. In the case of option 1, if God is immoral, then he is not God. Though at times the Bible attributes monstrous acts to God, there has to be another explanation for these wicked portrayals of God. If not, then we have an immoral God, and that is an impossibility given what we know of God's character in Jesus.

So when God seemingly approves of genocide, there has to be another explanation. How could a Christlike God ever commit an evil crime such as slaughtering people?

Option 2 is also unacceptable. We cannot say that God used to kill off nations, but God doesn't do that anymore. God cannot change in his moral personhood, because God is complete and fully formed perfection. Though things around God change, and we as a human race evolve, God is the same yesterday, today, and forever more (Malachi 3:6; Hebrews 13:8).

This leaves us with only one option—we need to read the Bible differently than with a flat-text reading. We really have no other choice, as the first two options are an assault on the character of God. They are in complete and utter conflict with the revelation of God as seen in Jesus.

This is why we need to learn how to read the Bible through a Jesus lens. Through a Jesus lens, we are able to state beyond a shadow of a doubt that any depiction of God in the Bible that is inconsistent with what God looks like, as seen in Christ, is inaccurate or incomplete. At the same time, having a Jesus lens allows us to uphold the conviction that the Bible is inspired by God. As we submit to Christ, we realize that Jesus himself believed in the inspiration of Scriptures. When tempted by Satan in the desert, Jesus quotes Scripture to defeat him. When challenged by his opponents, Jesus uses Scripture to oppose them. In confirming his credentials as the Son of God, he turned to the Bible to back up his claims. At other times, Jesus appealed to Scripture to challenge the way his adversaries understood what the Scriptures said. Battles over how to read Scriptures were a major source of contention between Jesus and the Pharisees and teachers of the law throughout his ministry. This ongoing feud served as a backdrop to the ministry of Jesus, and shows the high regard Jesus had for Scripture. At the same time, it shows that Jesus read Scripture differently than the religious experts of his day.

We can learn a lot about how a Jesus lens works from the way that Jesus studied Scripture.

Like Frederick Douglass, it appears that Jesus held to a hermeneutic of love in reading the Bible. We see this in Luke 4:18-30 when Jesus returns to his hometown synagogue. With great fanfare, Jesus is handed a scroll containing Isaiah 61:1-2. This is what he read: "The Spirit of the Lord is on me, because he has anointed me to proclaim good news to the poor. He has sent me to proclaim freedom for the prisoners and recovery of sight for the blind, to set the oppressed free, to proclaim the year of the Lord's favor" (Luke 4:18-19).

Interestingly, Jesus intentionally left out a significant part of what Isaiah had written. Here is the Isaiah text Jesus read from in its entirety: "The Spirit of the Sovereign LORD is on me, because the LORD has anointed me to proclaim good news to the poor. He has sent me to bind up the brokenhearted, to proclaim freedom for the captives and release from darkness for the prisoners, to proclaim the year of the LORD's favor *and the day of vengeance of our God*" (Isaiah 61:1-2).

Notice the words that Jesus left out: "and the day of vengeance of our God." Jesus failed to quote this line, choosing instead to stop right before it, ending with "to proclaim the year of the Lord's favor." Jesus and those who listened to him in the synagogue that day were very familiar with this messianic text.

They all knew it because it was a well-known biblical promise about a time when the Messiah of God would come and defeat Israel's enemies. As an occupied country, the Jews longed and prayed for the day when the Messiah would come and bring about the "day of vengeance of our God" on their enemy Rome. But Jesus conveniently left out the part about vengeance in Isaiah 61:2. He absolutely refused to quote it. The response of the crowd to this omission is very telling.

> Then he rolled up the scroll, gave it back to the attendant and sat down. The eyes of everyone in the synagogue were fastened on him. He began by saying to them, "Today this scripture is fulfilled in your hearing."
>
> All spoke well of him and were amazed at the gracious words that came from his lips. "Isn't this Joseph's son?" they asked. (Luke 4:20-22)

In the original language, "all spoke well of him" (v. 22) actually means "all bore witness to him."[7] Luke's description of the people as "amazed at the gracious words that came from his lips" (v. 22) does not necessarily mean they appreciated Jesus' words of grace, and instead could very well mean that they were amazed that Jesus didn't share the desire they possessed for the blood of Israel's enemies. No wonder we read that "the eyes of everyone in the synagogue were fastened on him" (v. 20). Perhaps they even made fun of him by calling him a nobody who was just a son of a lowly carpenter named Joseph (v. 22)?

One indication that the crowd around Jesus was upset with his omission of the vengeance portion of the Isaiah prophecy is seen in Jesus' response to them. He seems to scold them in verses 23-27. He refers to Scripture that describes the way that God graciously performed miracles for Gentiles at the expense of God's own chosen people. This instantly stirs up the crowd even further, and we read that they were "furious" with him. They actually formed a mob and tried to kill him because of his words (vv. 28-29). And what was it that made them so upset? Jesus had a hermeneutic of love. In contrast to the vengeance-seeking messiah they read about in Isaiah 61:2, Jesus represented a peaceful, life-giving, gracious Savior for all people, including those deemed to be the enemies of Israel.

There are other instances where Jesus reads Scripture in a more loving, nonviolent way. We see him purposely reinterpreting Scripture, as is evidenced in the way he challenges portions of the Mosaic Law that support hate, violence, and retribution (Matthew 5:21-44). In Matthew 5:45, he even takes a stab at Deuteronomy 28:24, a passage that his fellow Jews (and many Christians today) believe speaks of a retributive God who, in this passage, curses the unrighteous with drought until they are destroyed. In response to this view of God, Jesus turns that Scripture on its head and teaches the opposite. In his Sermon on the Mount Jesus claims that God is a non-vengeful Father who chooses to bless the righteous and the unrighteous alike, by sending them rain for their crops.

These aren't the only examples. In Luke 9, Jesus' disciples face opposition by Samaritans and ask Jesus if they should call fire down on them as a judgment from God. This request is not so strange when we consider the degree to which the Samaritans were despised by the Jews, and also that there is some biblical precedent for such action in Elijah's similar act of vengeance through calling down fire on Samaritans (2 Kings 1:9-14). Elijah's actions were obviously what the disciples were referring to when they wanted to enact God's wrath on the Samaritan village that had rejected them. Yet Jesus strongly rebukes them for even thinking of such a deed. Once again, Jesus rejects biblical violence to follow his peaceful way of interpreting Scripture.

And there is more. When an adulterous woman is dragged before Jesus to be stoned for her sin, Jesus defends her by saying, "Let any one of you who is without sin be the first to throw a stone at her" (John 8:7).

By saying these words, Jesus sets up a brand-new ethic that affirms life-giving mercy in complete opposition to the Old Testament law that supported the death penalty for various sins, including this sexual sin.

Jesus continues in his unique way of interpreting Scripture through his lens of love when he responds to the disciples of John the Baptist, who ask Jesus if he is the Messiah.

> When the men came to Jesus, they said, "John the Baptist sent us to you to ask, 'Are you the one who is to come, or should we expect someone else?'"
>
> At that very time Jesus cured many who had diseases, sicknesses and evil spirits, and gave sight to many who were blind. So he replied to the messengers, "Go back and report to John what you have seen and heard: The blind receive sight, the lame walk, those who have leprosy are cleansed, the deaf hear, the dead are raised, and the good news is proclaimed to the poor." (Luke 7:20-22)

In his answer, Jesus turned to Scripture to prove his messiahship, quoting from Isaiah and 1 and 2 Kings. In these quotations, Jesus tells John's disciples to let John know that the blind receive sight (Isaiah 29:18; 35:5; 61:1-2), the lame walk (Isaiah 35:6), lepers are cleansed (2 Kings 5:1-27), the deaf hear (Isaiah 29:18; 35:5), dead people are raised to life (1 Kings 17:17-34), and the poor receive good news (Isaiah 29:19). However, just as in Luke 4, Jesus intentionally skips the wrathful portions of the above Scriptures. For example, Jesus quotes Isaiah 29:18-19, which is all about the deaf hearing and the blind seeing, but he intentionally leaves out verse 20, which states, "The ruthless will vanish, the mockers will disappear, and all who have an eye for evil will be cut down."

Jesus also appeals to Isaiah 35:5-6, which speaks about the blind, deaf, and lame receiving healing, but once again, he deliberately leaves out verse 4: "Your God will come, he will come with vengeance; with divine retribution he will come to save you."

It is very clear from these examples that Jesus' unique way to read the inspired Scriptures is very different from a simple flat-text method of reading. As hard as this might be for some Christians to embrace, Jesus clearly challenged, reinterpreted, or seemingly disregarded portions of the Bible that he judged to not measure up to God's nonviolent, gracious character. This is very difficult for many of us who were taught to only read the Bible as a flat text, but it certainly appears to not be the way Jesus read the Scriptures.

The main turning point for me when it came to reading the Bible was twofold. First of all, I could no longer agree with flat-text readings of un-Christlike portrayals of God. I could no longer ignore the implications of the claims of Jesus and the New Testament that state that the fullness of God abides in Jesus. With this in mind, I had to admit that any flat-text portrayals of God as vengeful and immoral were a complete contradiction of what Jesus claimed about himself, and this was a problem for me. How could Jesus make such claims about a loving God if they were not true?

Second, I came to realize that Jesus didn't read the Bible in the same manner as I was taught to read it. As we have seen, Jesus read inspired Scripture differently than with a flat-text approach. He had a unique hermeneutic of love and peace that he used in dealing with the problems of the way that God was portrayed in some portions of the Bible. So I had a choice to make. I could read the Bible like Jesus, or not like Jesus. As a follower of Jesus, I had no other option but to choose Jesus. Don't get me wrong. The flat-text reading is good and proper to a point, but that point ends when we come across any teaching or depiction of God that is inconsistent with our Christlike God.

Jesus' hermeneutic of love also seems to be the way the apostle Paul read Scripture. Remember that Paul, once known as Saul, was a homicidal Pharisee who led a movement to capture, imprison, and kill Christians (Acts 8:1, 3). His flat-text reading of Scripture supported his evil and murderous behavior. Since he believed that God was violent and vengeful toward God's enemies, it was easy for Saul to conclude that he should strike out against Christians who were, in his opinion, enemies of God. However, as Saul and his lynch mob journeyed to Damascus to arrest Christians, he encountered Jesus (Acts 9:1-19). It was here that Saul experienced the love of Christ and was overpowered by the gracious forgiveness he found in Jesus. Saul was forgiven for all the horrible things he had done. His encounter with Jesus transformed his life and, interestingly, also changed how he read Scripture. It seems that Saul, who took on the Greek name Paul, changed from a flat-text reading of Scripture to a Jesus lens hermeneutic. Everything he wrote is based on his new interpretation of the law, reflecting a hermeneutic based on a Jesus lens. This is why he was able to go back to the Old Testament and reinterpret its meaning to allow for the end of the law and the inclusion of the Gentiles into the family of God. This new hermeneutic also changed how he viewed people. Paul was once a persecutor of Christians but now he was a beloved brother of the very Christians he had mistreated, and was also a loving minister to the once-hated Gentiles. Only Jesus can transform such hatred into love, and only a Jesus lens can allow us to see the Bible in such a loving light.

Paul's use of a Jesus lens is evident in the way he, like Jesus, intentionally omits in his writings portions of Scripture that involve God's vengeance. A good example of this is seen in Romans 15:9-10. In these verses, Paul makes his case that God's mercy is graciously extended to Israel's hated enemies, the Gentiles, by quoting from the Old Testament. Here is what Paul writes to the Romans:

> That the Gentiles might glorify God for his mercy. As it is written:
> "Therefore I will praise you among the Gentiles;
> I will sing the praises of your name."
>
> Again, it says,
> "Rejoice, you Gentiles, with his people."

In verse 9, Paul is directly reciting Psalm 18:49 to show how the Gentiles will be blessed by God. However, he could easily be accused of taking this verse out of context, as the rest of Psalm 18 is full of God's vengeance and wrath against Gentiles! Yet Paul chooses to leave those bits out. In the next verse, Romans 15:10, Paul goes further in describing the Gentile's joy at receiving God's mercy by quoting from Deuteronomy 32:43. Once again, Paul conveniently leaves out all the other verses in the passage that describe God's vengeance on his enemies, including the Gentiles. Like Jesus, Paul purposefully leaves out the violent portrayals of God.

In Ephesians 6, Paul once again adopts a loving, nonviolent hermeneutic in reading the Bible when he describes how we are to put on the armor of God. As Paul wrote these words, he was undoubtedly thinking of Isaiah 59:16-18, which describes God as wearing similar armor to pour out his wrath on living, breathing sinners. Yet Paul transforms this passage about God's wrath toward people by referring to the armor we are to wear as resources in our fight against evil. Unlike in the Isaiah passage, Paul clearly draws the line against using this armor for violence against other humans, as he points out that the evil we are to fight is "not against flesh and blood, but against the rulers, against the authorities, against the powers of this dark world and against the spiritual forces of evil in the heavenly realms" (Ephesians 6:12).

Both Jesus and Paul had a unique way of reading the Bible. It appears that they followed a flat-text reading of Scripture until their Jesus lens detected something ugly that was attributed to God. Once they came across anything that did not fit the character of a loving, gracious, nonviolent, Christlike God, they would take another direction in understanding what the Bible is really trying to say. Both Jesus and Paul seem quite comfortable skipping past certain verses that portray God in a negative light, choosing to emphasize other verses that uphold God in a Christlike manner. Sometimes they even do this with the same passage of Scripture! Yet both Jesus and Paul believed that the Bible was truly inspired by God. So this leads us to a very difficult question. If the Bible is inspired, then how can Jesus and Paul so easily move away from a simple, flat-text reading? Were Jesus and Paul cherry-picking verses they liked and omitting others they didn't like? If this is the case, did they disregard portions of Scripture as false and not inspired? In the next chapter we will attempt to answer these important questions by understanding that the key foundation in understanding the Bible is Jesus Christ.

QUESTIONS TO DISCUSS

Read Luke 4:14-30

1. Were there any "lightbulb" moments that struck you as being very important from this chapter? If yes, why were they important to you?

2. What are ways that we have created God in our own image? What are the ramifications of creating God to be like us? What are the practical ramifications for the church if we create God to be just like us?

3. What do the homeboy Jesus and the mirror Jesus look like to you? Give examples.

4. How do false Jesuses infiltrate your life? How do they infiltrate the church? What can we do to protect ourselves from them?

5. Why is the real Jesus so challenging for us to follow? Which of the three Jesuses really love us? Why do you think this way?

6. Were you surprised about what you read about how Jesus and Paul interpreted Scripture? If yes, why was this such a surprise to you?

7. What is one thing you will do this week in light of what you learned from this discussion?

EIGHT

Jesus, Not the Bible, Is the Word of God

ONE SUREFIRE WAY to demonstrate my immense ignorance is to ask me to pick a valuable diamond ring or necklace from a jewelry store. I wouldn't have a clue where to start. However, I have enough sense and humility to ask questions of people who do. The first thing an expert would do to assess the value of the diamond would be to examine it with a jeweler's loupe, a lens that is held up to the jeweler's eye to magnify the diamond, allowing the jeweler to determine its quality.

The Bible is like a diamond that must be studied through a specific lens to understand all its angles, contours, reflections, and various colors to establish its clarity. When reading Scripture, the lens of Jesus acts as our jeweler's loupe, helping to clarify what we are reading, especially the many challenging passages in the Bible.

The importance of having a Jesus lens is summed up in the following quote: "What if truth is not just a point of view . . .

not just a list of rules—yours, ours, or anyone else's? What if truth is not the ever-changing consensus of the crowd but instead is a person whom you get to know and who knows you. This person's story is told in the Bible. His name is Jesus."[1]

Jesus himself said; "I am the truth" (John 14:6).

Jesus as the truth of God certainly seems to be what the writer of the book of Hebrews was affirming when he wrote, "On many past occasions and in many different ways, God spoke to our fathers through the prophets. But in these last days He has spoken to us by His Son, whom He appointed heir of all things, and through whom He made the universe. The Son is the radiance of God's glory and the exact representation of his nature, upholding all things by His powerful word" (Hebrews 1:1-3 BSB).

In these powerful words we come to understand three things about God's revelation that make a Jesus lens indispensable to reading the Bible correctly:

1. JESUS IS THE ULTIMATE AND PRECISE REVELATION OF GOD

The writer of Hebrews tells us that Jesus is "the radiance of God's glory and the exact representation of his being" (NIV). If this is the case, then any question of what God is like is answered in the person of Jesus Christ. Knowing this truth is a foundational component of our Jesus lens, since it shines a bright light on any misconceptions we might have of God. This is especially important when we come across horrific descriptions of what God is like in the Old Testament. By accepting the fact that we have a Christlike God, we are forced to wrestle with passages that seemingly depict God as the complete opposite of what Jesus is like. When this happens, it is time to put on our jeweler's loupe, our Jesus lens, and look deeper into the passage to find the true meaning and value of what is written.

2. GOD'S REVELATION WAS INCOMPLETE PRE-JESUS

These verses in Hebrews also reveal to us that up to the time of Jesus, the Scriptures were not fully complete. The writer states that God's revelation came about on "many past occasions" and in "many different ways." The NASB translates these words as God speaking "in many portions." A portion is partial, not whole. Along these lines, J. B. Phillips translates these words as God giving "many different glimpses of the truth." When we think of this word *glimpse*, we understand it as seeing something briefly but not fully. The actual Greek word used in this passage is *polumerós*, which can be translated as "in many parts" (one at one time, another at another time, and so on). So we see that God provided partial revelations that acted as glimpses leading to the final truth and complete revelation of God, which is Jesus Christ.

3. GOD'S REVELATION IS COMPLETE THROUGH JESUS

The writer of Hebrews also tells us that God spoke through humans known as prophets, but that God now speaks to us "in these last days" through his Son. What an incredible statement to make. I like what Orthodox archbishop Dmitri Royster says concerning this phrase. "In these last days we understand that since Christ's coming into the world, no greater or further revelation can be expected and that the final period of history has begun."[2]

Jesus is the complete and full revelation of God. Since this is the case, doesn't it make sense that we utilize the Jesus lens when we read what inspired human authors wrote in the past? This is even more true considering that what these human authors wrote were just portions or partial glimpses of God's revelation. But now, with Jesus, we can understand the whole revelation of God. I believe Paul was pointing to this fact when he wrote that only Jesus can remove the veil that obscures our understanding of Scripture. "But their minds were made dull, for to this day the same veil remains when the old covenant is read. It has not been removed, because only in Christ is it taken away. Even to this day when Moses is read, a veil covers their hearts. But whenever anyone turns to the Lord, the veil is taken away" (2 Corinthians 3:14-16).

Christ reveals what the Scriptures say. This is why it is so important that we let Jesus interpret what the Bible says by reading the Scriptures through the lens of Jesus.

What do we learn from all of this? Matthew 23:10 sums it up: "You have one Instructor, the Messiah."

When it comes to reading the Bible, we need to allow Jesus to speak God's full truth to us by allowing a Jesus lens to guide us through the partial revelation of human writers. If we are to fully receive God's inspired words for us, we must have a Jesus lens. Without it, we are left to our own devices, and this can be very dangerous to ourselves and others.

The importance of reading the Bible through the lens of Jesus is further reinforced when we think of John's declaration that Jesus, not the Bible, is the true Word of God. "In the beginning was the Word, and the Word was with God, and the Word was God. He was with God in the beginning. . . . *The Word became flesh* and made his dwelling among us. We have seen his glory, the glory of the one and only Son, who came from the Father, full of grace and truth" (John 1:1-2, 14).

The Bible never claims to be the Word of God, but it does say that Jesus is the Word of God.

Since Jesus, not the Bible, is the capital *W* Word of God, doesn't it make sense to read the Bible through the lens of Jesus? Shouldn't Jesus, who is the very Word of God, have final say when it comes to how we read the Bible as the word of God? In fact, Jesus himself was very comfortable in taking authority over the way Scripture was to be read and understood. In the Sermon on the Mount, Jesus had no problem confronting Scriptures. In fact, Jesus openly challenges Old Testament Scripture no fewer than six times during the sermon. In Matthew 5, Jesus says, "You have heard that it was said to the people long ago, 'You shall not murder, and anyone who murders will be subject to judgment.' *But I tell you* that anyone who is angry with a brother or sister will be subject to judgment" (Matthew 5:21-22).

"You have heard that it was said, 'You shall not commit adultery.' *But I tell you* that anyone who looks at a woman lustfully has already committed adultery with her in his heart" (vv. 27-28).

"It has been said, 'Anyone who divorces his wife must give her a certificate of divorce.' *But I tell you* that anyone who divorces his wife, except for sexual immorality, makes her the victim of adultery, and anyone who marries a divorced woman commits adultery" (vv. 31-32).

"Again, you have heard that it was said to the people long ago, 'Do not break your oath, but fulfill to the Lord the vows you have made.' *But I tell you*, do not swear an oath at all" (v. 33-34).

"You have heard that it was said, 'Eye for eye, and tooth for tooth.' *But I tell you*, do not resist an evil person. If anyone slaps you on the right cheek, turn to them the other cheek also" (vv. 38-39).

"You have heard that it was said, 'Love your neighbor and hate your enemy.' *But I tell you*, love your enemies and pray for those who persecute you, that you may be children of your Father in heaven" (vv. 43-45).

Each time Jesus uses these words, "But I tell you," he is taking authority over the Old Testament Scriptures by adding more to it in unprecedented ways that override what is written. This is a clear example of the capital *W* Word of God, Jesus, having authority over the small *w* word of God.

These examples of Jesus overruling Old Testament commandments lead to a major conundrum: How do we handle verses that Jesus seems to redefine?

Along these same lines we also must ask, How do we handle representations of God in the Bible that are completely opposite of what Christ, as God in the flesh, is like?

The only way we can answer these questions is to go back to our Jesus lens and dig deeper into those passages that are at odds with Jesus' teachings and character. If at any time you can't find a deeper Christlike meaning in what you are reading, then there is only one option left—take Jesus' life and words over everything else, for he "is the radiance of God's glory and the exact representation of his being, sustaining all things by his powerful word" (Hebrews 1:3).

In other words, stick to Jesus no matter what. Even if the Bible seemingly contradicts Jesus' words or life example and it is a struggle to make sense of this, we must commit to Jesus, who is the living, capital *W* Word of God. A great example of how we must accept Jesus' words and life as the final authority when it comes to understanding the Bible is seen in the story of the transfiguration (Matthew 17:1-8). In this story Jesus takes Peter, James, and John up a mountain to be by themselves. When they reach their destination, Jesus becomes transfigured before their very eyes. While this happens, Moses and Elijah also appear and join Jesus in conversation. It is very important to understand the symbolism in this strange encounter. Moses and Elijah, as representatives of the law and prophets, embody the Scripture. In keeping with the typical Middle Eastern practice of hospitality, Peter takes responsibility to honor Moses, Elijah, and Jesus by asking to build them shelters. Peter says, "Lord, it is good for us to be here. If you wish, I will put up three shelters—one for you, one for Moses and one for Elijah" (v. 4).

Peter is thinking that this is a great opportunity for him to be able to learn not only from his Rabbi, Jesus, but also at the feet of Moses and Elijah. By doing this Peter is placing Moses, Elijah, and Jesus on the same level. In his mind, these three teachers have equal authority when it comes to speaking God's words. However, in response to Peter's intentions, God speaks out, saying, "This is my Son, whom I love; with him I am well pleased. Listen to him!"

And while God speaks, Moses and Elijah disappear, and only Jesus is left.

Why would God say to listen to Jesus and not mention Moses or Elijah? It is because God was declaring to Jesus' inner circle that Jesus has authority over these great teachers.

God is declaring this to us today: "Listen to him!"

We are wise to take God's advice to heed Jesus in all circumstances, including when we read the Bible. And, at those times when the Bible seemingly contradicts the life and teachings of Jesus, we must simply trust Jesus and listen to him above all else.

As Christians, we are people who proclaim, "Jesus is Lord!" This means that Jesus must be Lord of everything, including the Bible. I often come across people who claim to be committed followers of Jesus but who gladly put the Bible ahead of Jesus. This is especially the case when I am challenged by Christians who oppose active pacifism. It's strange how people who claim that Jesus is Lord over their lives will deny Jesus by using Scripture to argue against Jesus' very words about loving our enemies, turning the other cheek, and walking the extra mile. I often joke with these people by saying, "When Jesus said we need to love our enemies, I don't think he meant we should drop bombs on them." However, the most common response I hear is something like this, "Well, Colin, you mustn't forget that the God in the Old Testament ordered Israel to kill their enemies. So the Bible says it's okay to go to war!"

By taking this view, these people are arguing against Jesus and his teachings, which should never be the case if Jesus is truly Lord of their lives. Not to mention their "Marcion" tendencies to split God into two separate beings, since they talk about the God of the Old Testament. This way of reading Scripture over and above Jesus' teachings (which are also found in Scripture) places the small *w* words of the Bible ahead of the big *W* Word of God, Jesus Christ. In these kinds of disagreements between the word of God versus the true Word of God, we have only two options regarding to whom we will listen—Jesus or the Old Testament? I choose to heed what God the Father said on that mountaintop so many years ago: "Listen to Jesus." This applies to so many other themes, like the death penalty, slavery, women in ministry, and other pressing issues. "Listen to Jesus." After all, who has more authority than Jesus? Human prophets like Elijah? Moses and the law? Or the very Word of God himself? This is why we must always rely on Jesus to understand the Bible, and it is why we need a Jesus lens, for the true Word of God himself guides and leads us through the Bible.

In Hebrews 4, we read the following:

> For the word of God is living and active and sharper than any two-edged sword, even penetrating as far as the division

of soul and spirit, of both joints and marrow, and able to judge the thoughts and intentions of the heart. And there is no creature hidden from His sight, but all things are open and laid bare to the eyes of Him to whom we must answer.

Therefore, since we have a great high priest who has passed through the heavens, Jesus the Son of God, let us hold firmly to our confession. (vv. 12-14 NASB)

Like many, I used to believe that Hebrews 4:12-14 was describing the Bible as the written word of God, but I have now come to believe that this passage is referring to Jesus as the Word of God. The Word of God as depicted in this passage possesses personal qualities such as the ability to see, be alive and active, and judge. A book can't do these things, but a person can. This passage also says that "there is no creature hidden from His sight." Whose sight? Jesus' or a book's? The text also uses personal pronouns like *his* and *him*, once again pointing to a person, not to ink and paper. Finally, it is important to notice that the text says that all these personal attributes connect to our great High Priest, Jesus the Son of God. There is no doubt that this Word of God is Jesus.[3]

And what does this Word of God do? The text makes it clear—Jesus, the Word of God, guides us to truth by cutting deep into our soul and spirit, judging the thoughts and intentions of our heart. Best of all, we read that all things are open and laid bare to his eyes. Having Jesus as our great High Priest and true Word of God is a terrific way to read the Scriptures.

If we seek to be followers of Jesus, we must submit to the authority of Christ. This means we must read the Bible through a Jesus lens. In doing so we place our trust in the authority of Jesus to filter everything we read in the Bible concerning God and his ways, exactly in accordance to what Jesus is like. It is a wonderful opportunity to humbly welcome Jesus to join and lead us on our own "road to Emmaus" experiences each time we read the Bible. Through the lens of Jesus, we can join Cleopas and his friend and encounter what they experienced when they said to each other, "Were not our hearts burning within us while he talked with us on the road and opened the Scriptures to us?" (Luke 24:32).

QUESTIONS TO DISCUSS

Read Matthew 17:1-8

1. Were there any "lightbulb" moments that struck you as being very important from this chapter? If yes, why were they important to you?

2. How does Jesus change the way we read the Bible?

3. How is the Bible like a diamond to you? How do the diamond-like qualities of the Bible make it unique and different from other books? What does this tell you about the Bible?

4. In what ways is Jesus the true Word of God? As the Word of God, in what way does Jesus have authority over the Bible? Does this make the Bible less inspired or even more inspired by God?

5. In what ways might we overlook the authority of Jesus when reading the Bible?

6. What is one thing you will do this week in light of what you learned from this discussion?

NINE

Reading the Bible through a Jesus Lens, Part One

EVERY ONE OF US brings our own presuppositions to our understanding of what we read in the Bible. This is why we can find a wide variety of interpretations on the same passages. To help us clear up this confusion, we need an outside authority that can help us work through our own personal biases toward what we are reading in the Bible. This is where a Jesus lens comes in. But how does this Jesus lens work? How do we operate a Christ-centered jeweler's loupe so that Jesus opens the Scriptures to us?

A good example of how important it is to have a Jesus lens is found in a recent sermon I heard from a very highly esteemed preacher who reads the Bible without a Jesus lens. I share this with you as an example of the importance of reading Scriptures correctly. In his sermon, this pastor defended earlier comments he had made in which he declared that God hates us because we are sinners. The certainty of his belief in God's loathing toward us was based on Psalm 5:5-6 taken from the English Standard Version of the Bible, from which the pastor was preaching. "The boastful shall not stand before your eyes; *you hate* all evildoers. You destroy those who speak lies; the LORD abhors the bloodthirsty and deceitful man."

This Scripture, when read as a flat text, does state that God hates all evildoers. Not only that, but it claims that God destroys those who speak lies and abhors bloodthirsty and deceitful men. This pastor claimed to only be stating what the Bible says. Since we are all guilty of doing evil, lying, and being deceitful, he argued that God really does hate us and has every right to destroy us. After all, this is exactly what these words say when read with a flat reading of the Bible.

However, if you read this passage through a Jesus lens, you will be left with many questions, and that is a good thing because questions lead to truth. In this case, your Jesus lens would have detected that you are looking at a counterfeit diamond, as you would see the great contradiction between God's apparent hatred toward sinners and Jesus' great love of sinners, which would immediately raise questions like the following:

- Since Jesus is the exact representation of God, how can a Christlike God hate people?
- Is God even capable of hating people?
- Since Jesus loved sinners and enjoyed being in their presence by eating and drinking with them, why would this passage state that God hates, abhors, and seeks to destroy

sinners? Jesus certainly did not act this way toward sinners, so how could God view sinners in such an opposite way from Jesus?

- Jesus told us to love our enemies. Doesn't this command apply to God as well?

By not reading this passage through a Jesus lens, the pastor was unable to ask these important questions of the text, as he was unable to see the beautiful angles, colors, and contours within the diamond of this passage that only a Jesus lens can reveal.

With the help of a Jesus lens, this pastor would have seen that the description of God he was reading was un-Christlike, and this would have tipped him off to the need to dig deeper into the text, where he would discover that God is not saying he hates, abhors, and wants to destroy sinners and liars. He would understand that these are David's words about God, not God's words about himself. Oftentimes, the Psalms act as a kind of diary for David, where he has the freedom to lash out in anger in sharing his own human struggles and prayers and even project his own personal feelings of what he wishes God is like. In this specific case, David is going through a rough patch with people who have done him evil, lied about him, and even caused bloodshed in their pursuit of David. In his current state of distress, David wants God to take revenge on his opponents. When we understand the context of this psalm, we cannot blame David for feeling the way he does. We have all gone through troubling and hurtful experiences where we have felt the pain of being treated unfairly. It is in these times of vulnerability that we might lash out at our opponents, wishing that God would join our cause by hating, abhorring, or even destroying our adversaries. If you were to go back through your own diary from a time when you experienced great suffering because of being mistreated by others, it might read very similarly to what David wrote here in Psalm 5:5-6. And that is the point, isn't it? We are reading part of David's diary, and what we read are David's words and wishes, not God's.

Now let's go back to our hiking metaphor to reflect on this passage in Psalms. This pastor started out along the well-marked trail by following the surface meaning, or flat-text reading, of Scripture. He started well until he came across something that should have alarmed him—in this case, words that state that God hates us. Unfortunately, without a Jesus lens, this pastor was unable to be sensitive to the Holy Spirit alerting him to take a side trail that he needed to explore. If he had a Jesus lens, he would know that the psalmist's words could not be an accurate description of God.

By reading this passage through a Jesus lens, and accepting the inspiration of Scripture, there are many divine insights we can gain from these verses. By recognizing how David misrepresented God's character, we are alerted to the fact that we can often do the same thing. Like David, we can too easily wish harm on those who hurt us because we also tend to project our own sinful emotions onto God. David's very human example teaches us how we must be careful, as it is very easy for us to misconstrue God as being on our side as a justification for hate. Yet throughout all of this, we also learn that God patiently allows David to spew out his harmful thoughts, even if they make God look bad. God is willing to accommodate David's mischaracterization of who he is and is graciously willing to work with David in becoming a better man. We come to understand that we are all involved in a lifelong struggle to understand who

God is, and David helps us relate to this arduous process in our own lives.

I am thankful for the humanity present in divine inspiration. It brings me great comfort to know that God chose to communicate to us through fallen people like David and to reveal his grace to all of us who struggle to know God. We gain a great wealth of inspired truth from David's diary when we read it through a Jesus lens.

When I think of this, I am reminded of the great philosophical anthropologist René Girard, who masterfully describes Scripture by saying, "The Bible is a text in travail."

For Girard, the Bible is an inspired story of broken people trying to understand who God is and how God lovingly reaches out to them, slowly bringing them to the point where they can embrace the truth about themselves and God. We learn so much from this divine story found in our Bible, involving serious sinners, and a God who patiently journeys with them to bring them to a knowledge of his great love. In the Bible we see God's restorative and salvific mission as a back-and-forth struggle to bring fallen people to an understanding of their worth and God's true character. The Bible reveals a tug-of-war between good and evil, murder and love, hatred and grace, foggy misunderstanding and clear inspiration. Often, during this labor of redemption, God has to take a pastoral approach by starting with people right where they are, not where he would like them to be, to bring them along to the point where they can embrace truth. In this way, God willingly stoops down to humanity's level of depravity to work with us where we are at to bring us from despair to life. The Bible is an inspired story of this reality, and because of this, Girard is correct in saying the Bible is in travail as a God-breathed, living document about the condition of humanity and the love of God at work among us.

When I think of the Bible as being a book in travail concerning God's love for fallen humanity, I can't help but think of a story about missionaries who were sent to an indigenous community that performed the ritual of female genital mutilation. Even though this missionary couple detested this horrible practice, they decided to accommodate it for the time being. In fact, they actually decided to assist the practitioners of this ritual in performing it! How could they do such a horrible thing? Their answer is that they did it because they loved the community and the young girls who had to endure such a terrible experience. These missionaries decided that the most loving thing they could do was to meet the community where they were at and slowly work with them to help them see the inhumanity of this practice, which had been an accepted custom of their culture for hundreds of years. These missionaries wisely understood they could not expect the village to change their ways overnight. This was especially the case considering that the missionary couple were strangers who had just entered the community's culture. Trust had to be built, and this took time and excruciating patience. To change established cultural practices, these missionaries would have to work slowly with the community, beginning where the community was at. So they started gradually by bringing painkillers for the girls who endured the procedure. They also equipped the practitioners with better germ-free blades to perform the ritual, since many girls were dying of diseases or infections from unsanitary knives. Eventually, the missionaries were able to build up enough trust to slowly guide the tribe away from circumcising young girls. After many years of the missionaries' loving, accommodating presence, female genital cutting ended.[1]

This is what God, the perfect missionary, does in the Bible. Out of his love for Israel and his desire to remain in relationship with them, he is willing to accommodate their ways. Even if their ways are sinful, God stoops down to their level to bring them from great darkness to the light of Christ. This wonderful story of a loving God working with fallen humanity is recorded in the Bible as a book in travail. In light of this exciting yet tumultuous state of the Bible, it is imperative to have a Jesus lens to guide us through the whirlwind of Scripture so that we understand God's inspired words amid the story of humanity's ongoing struggles and God's gracious response.

Once people appreciate this reality about the Bible, they are better equipped to understand that not everything we read on the surface of Scripture about God is accurate. We have already seen how this is true when we looked at Psalm 5:5-6. When we say that the Bible is God-breathed,[2] we need to see its inspiration as involving fallen humans whose words, when read with a Jesus lens, might not reflect God's desires. Yet God still works with us, and his inspiration can be seen in the way God responds to fallen humans as reflected in the messiness of Scripture. Inspiration manifests itself in God's desire to communicate his ongoing love by patiently working within broken humanity to slowly bring us to the life God wants us to live. The stories in the Bible reveal sinners and a God who never demands that we embrace every aspect of his perfect will right away. God knows that in our fallen state, we cannot handle his wonderful truth all at once, so God lovingly brings us along at a pace we can take, carrying us toward the way of life God has always wanted us to live.

Jesus said, "I am the way and the truth and the life. No one comes to the Father except through me" (John 14:6). Jesus is the way, the truth, and the life. So his way must be our way, and his kingdom reign of love must be our truth and life. A Jesus lens always directs us in the way of truth and life. Knowing that the Bible contains a blow-by-blow account of God accommodating and wrestling with Israel to shape them to be his people reinforces our need for a Jesus lens to clarify God's truth within this sacred story. The Old Testament is an account of God wrestling with Israel to move them toward the way of Jesus (truth and life), even as they struggle to get there.[3] A Jesus lens helps us cut through this struggle so that we don't accept any erroneous concepts of God such as the one we saw in Psalm 5:5-6, or inappropriate social behaviors like slavery, polygamy, and others that are present in a flat-text reading of the Bible.

One way to understand the Bible is to see it as a witness to a living drama or an ongoing dance, with God as a master dance instructor who patiently labors alongside a clumsy, stubborn dance partner who has no desire to learn how to dance. God scoops us up in his loving arms and slowly works on us to give us a love for dance. He even allows us to step on his toes throughout this whole process while slowly teaching us the proper moves in God's waltz of righteousness. In this way the Bible gives witness to God patiently working with humanity, beginning where we are at and progressively revealing his truth to us in accordance to our ability to receive it. Paul describes this dance of progressive revelation well when he writes, "For now we see in a mirror dimly, but then face to face; now I know in part, but then I will know fully, just as I also have been fully known" (1 Corinthians 13:12 NASB).

If you have ever been to a dance studio, you will notice large clear mirrors stretching along the sides of the walls. These mirrors are used to reflect the dancers as they are performing so they can see whether their moves are correct. What Paul is saying is that there are lots of dance steps we need to learn, but the mirror we currently look into while learning these steps can be blurry.[4] In applying this dance studio image to the verse above, we can say that the Scriptures are truth, but they are not fully clear to us. This is why we need a Jesus lens to clarify what we are reading.

When Paul wrote these words about seeing Christ face-to-face rather than through a mirror, he was referring to a time when Christ returns and all will be made clear to us. But this verse also reveals the limited nature of our minds. Paul is stating that our inadequate minds cannot entirely behold the fullness of God and his truth. This is why God has to accommodate to our weaknesses. God can only reveal his truth gradually, in accordance to our ability to accept God's truth. This inevitably slows us down as we struggle to fully know the right dance moves. However, in Christ Jesus we have the full and final revelation of God. Jesus is the perfect dance partner, and he wants to dance with us when we read the Bible so that we can understand what it truly means. It's a slow process, but with Jesus as our dance partner and instructor, we will get there.

Only God can disclose his truth to us, and he does so through progressive revelation that leads to Jesus. This revelation is built one dance step at a time so that our limited minds are capable of taking in what God is revealing to us. To illustrate how this revelatory dance works, let's go back to this issue of slavery in the Bible. Oppressing people as captives is not what God wants for us in any shape or form, yet a flat-text reading of most of the Old Testament leaves us with the impression that it is acceptable. Why is this? To answer this question, we must understand that God had to start the dance of freedom with an ancient culture steeped in a history of slavery that saw "through a glass darkly." God had no choice but to work with people where they were at in order to move them away from this horrible practice. To do this, God initially accommodated their blindness to the sin of enslaving people in order to begin the work of helping them change their evil ways and bringing them to the point where they would end slavery. This process is revealed in Scripture as progressive revelation, in which God slowly reveals his truth, in bits and pieces, in accordance to the culture's capacity to accept and act on God's revelation. In the case of slavery, its destructive dance was accepted as an ancient Middle Eastern social reality, and sadly, Israel adopted this evil just like the nations surrounding them.[5] So we see God accommodating slavery only as a starting point to slowly bringing Israel to the point of abolishing slavery, based on the increasing revelation of the dignity of human beings. This progressive revelation takes root, beginning with the instituting of God's laws regarding the ways in which slaves were to be cared for, laws that required the treatment of slaves to be far more humane than in the nations surrounding Israel. Slowly but surely, as Israel began to learn the proper dance steps of freedom, this progressive revelation built in tempo, becoming a glorious dance of freedom.

In the New Testament we read about Onesimus, a slave owned by a man named Philemon. Onesimus had escaped slavery and became a follower of Jesus while on the run from Philemon. Paul states that Onesimus has become his spiritual son and sends him back to his master with a handwritten letter telling Philemon to welcome Onesimus no longer as a slave but as a brother. Paul writes,

> Perhaps the reason he was separated from you for a little while was that you might have him back forever—*no longer*

as a slave, but better than a slave, as a dear brother. He is very
dear to me but even dearer to you, both as a fellow man and as
a brother in the Lord.

So if you consider me a partner, welcome him as you
would welcome me. (Philemon 1:15-17)

When you consider these words of Paul alongside what he
wrote in Galatians 3:28, it is clear that God does not approve of
slavery: "There is neither Jew nor Gentile, *neither slave nor free,*
nor is there male and female, for *you are all one in Christ Jesus.*"

Although the dance steps are clear, they can be very hard to
learn from within a culture steeped in slavery. But each dance
step points to Jesus. "You are all one in Christ Jesus."

Having a Jesus lens helps us see that God is leading humanity in a clear direction. God has entered already existing societal
structures and is lovingly changing them in a very positive and
significant way. Though Israel takes on slavery as a social norm,
God slowly introduces new dance steps to help them escape this
sin. Like a wise dance instructor, God slowly and patiently teaches
Israel the dance of freedom, bringing them from darkness to light
through progressive revelation. A Jesus lens helps us go back in
time and identify God's accommodations so that we can see God's
intended trajectory. If you settle with a flat-text reading, you will
miss out on the truth of where God is taking us.

Progressive revelation is also seen in the way that God accommodates the sacrificial system as part of Israel's worship.
God originally allows the sacrifice of animals, since Israel had
adopted this ancient Middle Eastern practice, believing strongly
in the cultic practice of the spilling of blood to appease God.
Knowing how committed Israel was to their belief in sacrificial
rituals, God allowed them to participate in this form of bloody

worship. However, it is interesting to note that this accommodation permitting animal sacrifice was a great step forward, since the nations surrounding Israel sometimes sacrificed human beings as part of their worship.

At the beginning of Israel's history, we read that God allows for the sacrifice of animals as part of their worship. "The LORD called to Moses and spoke to him from the tent of meeting, saying, "Speak to the sons of Israel and say to them, 'When anyone of you brings an offering to the LORD, you shall bring your offering of livestock from the herd or the flock'" (Leviticus 1:1-2 NASB).

This animal sacrificial system becomes a mainstay of Israel's worship. However, later we read Scriptures that contradict the importance of the sacrificial system, revealing that it was never really what God wanted.

> Sacrifice and offering you did not desire—
>   but my ears you have opened—
>   burnt offerings and sin offerings you did not require.
>   (Psalm 40:6)

> You do not delight in sacrifice, or I would bring it;
>   you do not take pleasure in burnt offerings.
>   (Psalm 51:16)

> For I desire mercy, not sacrifice,
>   and acknowledgment of God rather than burnt offerings.
>   (Hosea 6:6)

The prophet Jeremiah reveals God's accommodation of sacrifices as part of God's patient plan in guiding Israel to change from their wickedness to the righteous ways of God.

For I did not speak to your fathers, or command them in the day that I brought them out of the land of Egypt, concerning burnt offerings and sacrifices. But this is what I commanded them, saying, "Obey My voice, and I will be your God, and you will be My people; and you shall walk entirely in the way which I command you, so that it may go well for you." Yet they did not obey or incline their ear, but walked by their own advice and in the stubbornness of their evil hearts, and they went backward and not forward. Since the day that your fathers came out of the land of Egypt until this day, I have sent you all My servants the prophets, sending them daily, again and again. Yet they did not listen to Me or incline their ear, but stiffened their neck; they did more evil than their fathers. (Jeremiah 7:22-26 NASB)

Here Jeremiah has a deeper revelation and reveals the push and pull between God and Israel. God tries to influence Israel to do what is right, but Israel pushes against God's good ways. In this struggle we see that God allows for sacrifices to take place, even if he never intended for them to be part of Israel's worship. Surprisingly, God reveals that he never told Israel to sacrifice animals. In other words, burnt offerings and sacrifices were human ideas, not God's, which reveals that God accommodated their wishes.

Progressive revelation shows us that God never desired sacrifice, but wanted obedience and justice in its place as true acts of worship.[6] Clearly, sacrifices were an accommodation from God as part of his plan to meet Israel where they were at so he could slowly bring them to a better way of worship.

There are many more examples of progressive revelation in relation to God's loving accommodations in the Bible. One clear example of this is seen in Matthew 19:6-9 when Jesus explains that Moses permitted a simple form of divorce in his day because, at that time, the people's "hearts were hard." Then Jesus goes on to reveal God's true desire for marriage, which is very different from what Moses wrote in Deuteronomy 24:1-3. Clearly God accommodated because of the condition of people's hearts in Moses's day, and it is also another example of progressive revelation.

We also see God and his accommodating ways in God's willingness to allow Israel to have a king. God's intention for Israel was that he alone would always be their king, but we read in 1 Samuel 8:5 that the people of Israel demand that Samuel "appoint a king to lead us, such as all the other nations have."

Israel's heart was shaped by the culture around them to the point that they could not conceive of having God rule over them as their king. Though it is against God's wishes, he accommodates their desires and allows them to have a human king. The interesting thing about this accommodation is that God consents to it even though he knows it will lead to Israel's future suffering (see 1 Samuel 8). As with divorce, this was not God's will for Israel, but he accommodates their wishes.

This reality of God's patient accommodation to humanity is an important reason we need to be careful with surface readings of Scripture. If we accept a flat reading, we might be approving of something from which God wanted to free us! We must apply a Jesus lens to everything we read. In the past we have seen many horrible examples of settling for a surface reading of the Bible instead of using a Jesus lens to dig deep into the diamond mine of Scriptures. History is littered with examples of people who, through a simple flat-text reading, have accepted God's accommodations as justification for terrible things with which God does not agree. We can see how a flat reading of the Bible that does not take into account God's accommodations can conflict with a Jesus-lens reading of Scripture at work in the lives of two legendary evangelists who held completely opposite opinions about slavery based on their understandings of Scripture. One of these evangelists, Charles Finney, was an abolitionist. He was the first evangelist to introduce what we would today call altar calls, but his altar calls had a slight twist to them. Near the end of his sermons, Finney would ask anyone who wanted to accept Jesus as Lord and Savior to come forward and meet him at the altar for a time of prayerful repentance. After the new converts had come forward and prayed, Finney had them sign a commitment to the abolitionist cause. For Finney, being a follower of Jesus meant standing up against slavery. As a sign of true repentance, those who came forward had to promise to release any people they had enslaved and commit to the abolitionist cause as proof of their sincerity and commitment to Christ. Finney's Jesus-centered reading of the Bible led him to believe that being a Christian had serious social ramifications, including repudiating the horrible sin of slavery. Finney understood that the practice of slavery in the Old Testament was not God's will but an accommodation. Yet one hundred years before Finney was signing up new converts to join the abolitionist crusade, the revivalist Jonathan Edwards was himself a slave owner! Both of these men read from the same Bible, but they held completely opposite convictions when it came to slavery. This is a perfect example of our need for a Jesus lens to help us dig beneath the surface of the Bible. Edwards' flat reading of the Bible led him to accept slavery, but Finney's deeper, Jesus-focused method of reading Scripture led him to vehemently oppose the practice.

Although reading Scripture in this way might seem complicated, it really is not that complex. If we consistently refer back to Jesus and use him as our ultimate lens in reading Scripture, we will gain insight into what the Bible is truly saying. After all, the Bible is the word of God that always points to the true Word of God, Jesus.

QUESTIONS TO DISCUSS

Read Philemon

1. Were there any "lightbulb" moments that struck you as being very important from this chapter? If yes, why were they important to you?

2. How can we get into trouble if we limit our method of reading the Bible to a flat-text method only?

3. What does it mean to you to acknowledge the Bible as a book in travail?

4. What are some real-life examples of how you have seen accommodation as a loving and effective way to help people change?

5. What is one thing you will do this week in light of what you learned from this discussion?

TEN

Reading the Bible through a Jesus Lens, Part Two

A RECENT ARTICLE in the *Huffington Post* describes the challenge many believers have when they read Scripture.

> Some people stick to the Old Testament and love to use this phrase: "You can't pick and choose which parts of the Bible to follow." Ironically, this is something they themselves *must* do since the Old Testament has rules like not eating pork, not shaving your beard, not wearing clothes made from more than one animal, stoning adulterers, and killing disobedient children. Therefore, they must *pick and choose* which parts of the Old Testament they want to apply. If anyone tells you the Old Testament applies today, they are trying to get around the teachings of Christ.[1]

As we have seen, Jesus and the apostle Paul clearly had a different method of reading Scripture that went beyond a flat-text reading. For both, a hermeneutic of love was the foundation for reading the Bible. Jesus had special insight into the Scriptures since he is the true Word of God. Jesus embodied what the Father is like, and as Lord of all things, including the Bible, he was able to perfectly understand Scripture clearly and without any impediments. Perhaps this is what Paul alluded to when he wrote, "But their minds were made dull, for to this day the same veil remains when the old covenant is read. It has not been removed, because only in Christ is it taken away. Even to this day when Moses is read, a veil covers their hearts. But whenever anyone turns to the Lord, the veil is taken away" (2 Corinthians 3:14-16).

When Paul wrote these words, he might have been looking back to his years as a popular religious leader. From birth he was groomed to be a powerful teacher of the law. Born into a very religious family as a son of Pharisees (Acts 23:6), he was blameless under the law throughout his life (Philippians 3:4-6). His knowledge of Scripture was second to none, having received his education at the school of Gamaliel, one of history's preeminent rabbis (Acts 22:3). Yet Paul states that even in light of his elite religious pedigree and theological education, his mind was dull and weak in understanding the Scriptures. It was as if he, along with other flat-text readers of the Old Testament, had a thick veil covering his mind and heart, hampering his ability to understand the Bible. However, after he encountered Jesus on the road to Damascus, he experienced a God of love instead of a God full of divine wrath and condemnation. This encounter with a loving God transformed his heart and his way of reading the Bible. Now he was able to read the Scriptures through a Jesus lens, and that made all the difference.

FOUR COMPONENTS PRESENT IN READING THE BIBLE WITH A JESUS LENS

By using a hermeneutic of love, Jesus was able to intentionally avoid passages that clearly depicted God as a violent deity. It also allowed him to replace them with selected passages that spoke of the love and grace of the Father. This is hardly a traditional way to read the Bible, yet as we have seen, it was how Jesus read the Scriptures. This leads us to ask two questions. First of all, if we call ourselves followers of Jesus and recognize he is Lord of all, including Lord of the Bible, shouldn't we also follow his way of reading the Bible? Second, when we consider that Jesus had a high view of the Bible, yet read it in such a free manner, it must mean that his understanding of inspiration might very well be different from ours.

When considering Jesus and his hermeneutic of love, we can observe four components at work that allow him flexibility in reading the Bible while still being true to the inspiration of Scripture.

Component 1: *A Jesus lens reveals that inspiration leaves room for accommodation*

We have already highlighted the reality of this principal of accommodation that God uses to relate to his beloved children. All throughout the Bible, we see our missionary God willing to stoop to the level of understanding of his people and work with them to bring them along to his truth. Although teaching through accommodation might appear to be wrong, it is the basis for transformation. To help people change, we all have to start where they are at to slowly bring them to where they ought to be.

A childcare worker shared a story of how accommodation works from her experience of caring for a young girl who was a victim of countless forms of sexual abuse from her father.[2] For the first few weeks that this girl lived at the group home, she would intentionally defecate in her pajamas and place feces around her bed. When this happened the first few times, her caregiver asked her to make sure to go to the bathroom before she went to bed. However, each night this little girl continued to soil her bedroom, resulting in a nauseating stench. Naturally, this repetitive behavior upset her caregiver but in time, this little girl felt safe enough to share with her caregiver why she would repeatedly soil her bed. During one horrible episode of abuse in her past, she accidently defecated in her bed. This immediately put a stop to the abuse. Her perpetrator was repulsed by her actions and quickly left her room. The next night, when her abuser returned, she accidently soiled herself out of fear. Once again, her abuser immediately stopped what he was doing and quickly left her room. From that point on, the girl would intentionally soil her bed as a defense to prevent the abuse she was experiencing. And it worked. Upon hearing this explanation, her caregiver was no longer upset with the girl's defecation in her bed. In fact, for the next week or so, the caregiver put on gloves and joined the little girl in spreading her feces all around her room. By stooping down to the level of this hurting little girl, her caregiver was able to build the trust necessary to slowly steer her away from a life of fear to the point that she would no longer defecate in her bed.

In the Bible we see God do similar things, accepting us where we are at and slowly guiding us to where he wants us to be. At first, it might seem that God is accepting of our bad behavior, just like the caregiver who willingly spread feces all over a child's room, but there is a loving purpose behind such action. In stooping down to our level, God does not leave us there, but works with us to bring us along to where he wants us to be.

We see some of these acts of accommodation in Scripture when we come across horrible practices like slavery, polygamy, sexism, racism, and violence. There are many verses that, on a surface level, seem to support such evils, and it might even appear that God is approving of such things. However, God is not supportive of these practices at all, but stoops down to where we are at and begins there. Since love never forces people to change but instead uses influence to bring about personal transformation, God is willing to allow for our misconceptions and cultural sins so that he can slowly bring his beloved ones away from such depravity. By having a Jesus lens based on a hermeneutic of love, we can read deeper into these trouble-some passages to see what God is doing beneath the surface of these verses. Through accommodation, our Christlike God of peace is willing to put up with fallen humanity's sinful habits to lovingly break us free from such terrible behaviors, including, at times, mischaracterizations of God himself. If we stick to a surface reading of the Bible and do not accept the reality of an accommodating God, then we have to accept the various evils we read about as approved by God. Truth be told, most flat-text readers of the Bible go against their own simple hermeneutic when it comes to matters such as slavery. As Matthew Korpman so clearly states, "The reality is that almost every Christian in America today now agrees unanimously (without even thinking much about it) that the God they serve does not approve of slavery, even though the Bible is very clear that God did and by virtue of silence, should still. Even if they are not consciously aware of what they are doing, these Christians have made a decision to reject certain verses and accept others, all on the basis of the incarnate Jesus and the Spirit's moving upon their conscience."[3]

We can only reject accommodations like slavery if we have a Jesus lens, or as Korpman writes, "on the basis of the incarnate Jesus," since a flat reading supports such evils.

Component 2: A Jesus lens allows for a trajectory (progressive revelation) as part of inspiration

God's accommodation results in a forward trajectory in which God starts where people are at and moves them toward what is right. "The LORD is my shepherd" (Psalm 23:1), and as a good shepherd, he knows that to care for his sheep, he has to start where they are at (accommodation) and then move them forward in the right direction (trajectory). When reading the Bible, we don't just ask, "What does this say" and leave it at that. We also need to ask, "What is the trajectory of change on which God is working?" This is where the story of the Bible is going, and it is vitally important that we use our Jesus lens to see the trajectory. If we stick to a flat-text reading and do not use our Jesus lens to see this trajectory, we will miss out on the truth of where God is taking us, and we can find ourselves in all sorts of trouble.

Component 3: A Jesus lens allows for a cruciform hermeneutic in inspiration

Closely connected to God allowing for accommodation in order to move people forward in his divine plan of revelation is this idea of a cruciform interpretation of Scripture. This view states that the crucified Christ is the supreme revelation of God. On the cross we see God's love as Jesus willingly taking on the appearance of a criminal to bring us redemption. The argument is made that something similar happens when we look at disturbing portrayals of God in the Old Testament in which God stoops down in a great act of accommodation, willingly taking on the ugly appearance of what sinful people project him to be—a wrath-filled warrior God—in order to keep his covenant with his people. Once again, I refer to Greg Boyd in describing how a cruciform hermeneutic works. "By faith we see something else is going on behind the scenes of Jesus's crucifixion that sets him apart from all other crucified people. By faith, we look beyond surface appearances to behold God stooping an infinite distance out of love to bear our sin as this particular guilty-appearing, God-cursed criminal."[4]

Boyd continues, "The faith of believers lightens up what is going on behind the scenes of the crucifixion. It thus allows them to see through the ugly sin-mirroring surface of the cross to behold God stooping an infinite distance to enter into solidarity with our sin and to thereby take on an ugly appearance that mirrors this sin. This is why the cross is for believers both the revelation of the revolting ugliness of our sin and the revelation of the supremely beautiful God who was willing to stoop to take on this revolting ugliness."[5]

This principle of God's hidden revelation as seen on the cross can also be applied to Scriptures that portray God in such an un-Christlike manner. "The driving conviction of the Cruciform Hermeneutic," writes Boyd, "is that since Calvary gives us a perspective of God's character that is superior to what people in the Old Testament had, we can also enjoy a superior perspective of what was actually going on when the Old Testament authors depicted God engaging in and commanding violence."[6]

By applying what we now know about God's love as seen in the cross, we come to understand that "the Cruciform Hermeneutic enables us to discern the beauty of the crucified God rising out of portraits of God that on the surface appear profoundly ugly. The crucified Christ, in short, gives us the 'Magic Eye' to discern him in the depths of even the most horrific violent portraits of God."[7]

A cruciform hermeneutic argues strongly that what we see in the crucifixion of Jesus can also be seen when reading Scripture. To the casual observer who lived under Roman rule, Jesus appeared to be just like all the rest of the criminals who were crucified by Rome. However, those of us who are believers are able to look deeper into the meaning of the crucifixion of Jesus and see that something else is happening beneath the surface. This was not a typical crucifixion that took place under Roman rule. It was a loving act of God to defeat the powers of sin, Satan, and death. To use an oft-repeated phrase, "There's more to this than meets the eye."

On the cross, Jesus was willing to take on the form of a criminal in response to the ugliness of humanity's sin. However, when you dig deeper you no longer see a criminal; rather, you see a supreme divine lover who goes to great lengths to bring forgiveness and freedom to sinful humanity enslaved by the powers of evil. Similarly, when God is portrayed as violent or vengeful in the Bible, God is willing to take on that false appearance to work with sinful humanity to bring them to a true understanding of who he is. In both cases, with the cross and the Bible, God's revelation is revealed underneath the surface of initially disturbing appearances while, at the same time, God honors human freedom. So in the crucifixion, God grants freedom to sinners to act on their evil impulses, but at the same time God is able to work through sinful autonomy to reveal his great love. In the same way, biblical inspiration honors the freedom of human writers to hold to their own perspectives even if they describe God in an unworthy manner. Boyd writes, "Because God supremely values authentic agape-love relationships, and because he does not want to dehumanize people, he relies on influential rather than coercive power to accomplish his purposes. For this reason, I submit, God had to accommodate his self-revelation to the spiritual state and cultural conditioning of his people in the ages leading up to Christ. Only gradually could God change people's hearts and minds so that they could receive more and more truth about his true character and about his ideal will for them."[8]

Because of the incredible love of God as seen in Christ and the cross, we now have a more complete view of what God is like than the Old Testament writers ever had. Unlike the limitations of a flat-text reading, a cruciform hermeneutic allows us to apply what we now know about God to Old Testament passages that describe God in an un-Christlike manner. In this way, a cruciform hermeneutic helps us read deeper into inspired Scripture while also honoring who Jesus revealed the Father to be. This Jesus lens helps us unite both Old and New Testaments to function as a unified revelation from God that, in the words of Jesus, fulfills the law. As Derek Flood puts it, "As with the command to take an 'eye for an eye' this deeply rooted ethos of enemy-hate in God's name is likewise overturned in Jesus. Yet, Jesus does not regard any of this as abolishing the law, but as fulfilling it. He fulfills the law; and yet in order to do so, he utterly changes it. That is how Jesus understands faithfulness to Scripture. Fulfilling Scripture for Jesus means lovingly bringing it into its fully intended purpose."[9]

Bringing a Jesus lens to Old Testament passages that reveal God in an unworthy manner helps us fulfill inspired Scripture—or as Flood describes it, "Jesus lovingly brings it into its fully intended purpose."

Component 4: *A Jesus lens includes human voices in inspiration*

Closely connected to understanding the Bible through a cruciform hermeneutic is the ability to identify when a writing was not clearly from God and was deeply influenced by the author's perspective. It is important to realize that those who wrote the Scriptures were not simple robots who dictated every phrase, word for word, that God wanted them to write. Rather, God's Spirit illuminated the minds of Scripture's writers so that they could express God's salvation in their own words and through their own culture's forms of literature. Theologians call this the appropriation model of inspiration. Paul Copan and Matthew Flannagan write,

> The Bible can simultaneously be the word of God and the words of humans. So when a head of state commissions an ambassador to speak on her behalf (or when someone is given the power of attorney), that person doesn't become a mere mouthpiece. Rather, that representative chooses his own words—words that reflect his personality, character and knowledge (or perhaps lack of it)—even if they are not the precise words the head of state (or client) herself would have chosen. . . . Similarly, biblical interpretation can take into account all the particularities and styles of the human writers and still interpret what God said by that. The appropriation model also explains how one can accept that the

Bible is God's word without claiming that God necessarily affirms exactly what the human author affirms.[10]

In inspiring the writers of Scripture, God appropriates all sixty-six books written by various authors, in three languages, from varying backgrounds and cultures over a span of many years into one God-story—the Bible. God's appropriation of the stories of biblical writers into his story means that God doesn't necessarily affirm everything that the human author writes. For example, we can see Job's friends and even Job stating things that are not correct about God, yet they remain in the inspired text. Also, as we have seen, writers like David can lament the suffering they are going through by expressing their desires for God to punish their enemies in ways that God would never act. Yet when you put all of this human discourse together, God is able to make it his inspired book.

This blend of human authorship and divine inspiration is very evident when we consider Paul's writings. He acts as a good case study in which we can glean some understanding of how God works through human freedom in inspiring the writers of Scripture. In some of Paul's letters he admits that what he is writing is not from God but is based on his own opinion. In 1 Corinthians 7:12, Paul addresses the church in Corinth concerning the topic of marriage and openly admits that what he is writing is his own opinion: "To the rest I say this (I, not the Lord)." He does this again in 2 Corinthians 11:17 while defending his position as an apostle when he writes, "In this self-confident boasting I am not talking as the Lord would." In 1 Timothy 2:11-15, we come across this once again when Paul voices his opinion about women in the church. Many people have taken what he said as a hard-and-fast rule that limits women from taking leadership roles in the church. What they fail to recognize, or even notice, is that in verse 8, Paul starts his dialogue that leads to his take on the role of women by stating that he desires his readers to follow his ideals. In the Greek, this word for "desire" actually means "a personal desire." So Paul is admitting that what he is saying about women is coming from his own wishes, not necessarily from God. Here we can see that much of the argument used for limiting women in leadership comes from Paul's wishes within the certain context he is addressing and it is not the Lord's command in all circumstances.[11] This should make many people who believe women cannot hold leadership positions in the church pause and rethink their position.[12]

In 1 Corinthians 1:14-16 we come across very interesting verses that shine even more light on this process of divine inspiration. Paul writes, "I thank God that I did not baptize any of you except Crispus and Gaius, so no one can say that you were baptized in my name. (Yes, I also baptized the household of Stephanas; beyond that, I don't remember if I baptized anyone else)."

Paul's full humanity is seen in all its comic weakness as he stumbles over his memory in the midst of writing sacred Scripture, first claiming he never baptized anyone, then remembering he did baptize a few people, and then admitting there could be others he has completely forgotten about. The wonderful thing about all of this is that it reveals how God trusted and worked through humans to communicate his words and, at the same time, granted them freedom in how they wrote what they did. This is what divine inspiration looks like, and with this in mind we can see that God's view of biblical inspiration is much freer than a hypercontrolled understanding to which some people hold.

It is clear from the above examples that there is a very human dimension to our inspired Scriptures. It appears that God speaks through humans, and his meaning of inspiration allows them some latitude to speak from their own contextual viewpoint. Paul seemed to admit this and was self-aware of it in the passages we looked at above, and it seems that Jesus believed this as well. This is why Jesus often quotes the human side of inspiration by referring to Moses's role in some of the laws that Jesus challenged. As stated earlier, accommodation allows for human frailties that are not divine standards. This was seen in God's working with human weaknesses in allowing for a king and permitting divorce. We also see some interesting human freedom in John 7 when Jesus gets into trouble for his teaching and for breaking the law by healing on the Sabbath. Jesus says, "Has not Moses given you the law? Yet not one of you keeps the law. Why are you trying to kill me? . . . Yet, because Moses gave you circumcision (though actually it did not come from Moses, but from the patriarchs), you circumcise a boy on the Sabbath" (John 7:19, 22).

Jesus points to the human side of inspiration by emphasizing the role Moses had in giving the law. Interestingly, this inspired text also allows for the author of John (or a later scribe) to insert a comment into these verses, attempting to provide editorial clarity, when he writes, "Though actually it did not come from Moses, but from the patriarchs."

This again reveals to us the human side of the Bible, as we have an inspired writer editing the Bible.[13]

So what are we to make of all this? It seems that God's inspiration works with the human writers instead of overpowering them. Paul models this as he wrote of the tug-of-war he experienced between the divine perspective and his own personal opinions. He also recognized his human weakness when he revealed his memory loss concerning whom he baptized, all while writing inspired Scripture! Jesus also discloses times when Moses attributed his opinions to God, even though, according to Jesus, they were not directly God's desires. Yet in all of this, the Bible remains inspired. This is very different from a limited, flat-text view of inspiration.

QUESTIONS TO DISCUSS

Read 2 Corinthians 3:7-18

1. Were there any "lightbulb" moments that struck you as being very important from this chapter? If yes, why were they important to you?

2. How has your understanding of the inspiration of Scriptures changed after reading this chapter?

3. What are some questions, concerns, or encouragements you glean when you think of what you learned from this chapter concerning our inspired Scripture? How will this affect your Bible reading?

4. What is one thing you will do this week in light of what you learned from this discussion?

PART THREE

APPLYING A JESUS LENS TO TOUGH PASSAGES THAT QUESTION THE LOVE OF GOD

Rather than cry out for a more biblical world, I would rather suggest that we cry out for a more Christlike one. Why? Because a "biblical" world isn't necessarily a Christlike one. War, genocide, slavery, women-as-property and polygamy are all "biblical" ideas. But when re-evaluated in the light of Christ, such things fade into the background and are eclipsed by His radiance and glory.

—KEITH GILES
Jesus Unbound

ELEVEN

Understanding the Wrath of a Loving God

ONE OF THE CUTEST, yet strangest, toys I have ever seen for toddlers is a model of Noah's ark. The ones I have seen contain a smiling, bearded Noah with his family in tow, and a pile of really cute animals. Everyone looks so happy, including the animals. These Noah sets have it all—except for a few missing elements of the biblical story, such as a sneering mass of degenerate human malcontents, giant demonic Nephilim, and a massive flood that destroys them all. But the toy set is adorable as long as you ignore the missing pieces that populate the rest of the story.

When it comes to God's wrath as seen in the story of Noah's ark, many of us do our best to ignore the rest of the story. Why wouldn't we? After all, it is pretty gruesome. None of us can rejoice in a worldwide flood that drowns every living creature on the earth except for Noah's family and the chosen animals that entered the ark. One could possibly justify the destruction of an all-out sinful humanity, but what about the innocent infants who were drowned? Or how about all the animals that were destroyed? This doesn't make sense. We know that God cares for people and animals, as was reflected when he spoke to Jonah about not destroying Nineveh. "And should I not have concern for the great city of Nineveh, in which there are more than a hundred and twenty thousand people who cannot tell their right hand from their left—and also many animals?" (Jonah 4:11)

Yet in the case of the Noahic flood, babies and even animals were destroyed alongside fallen humanity.

When you include this story alongside others like that of Sodom and Gomorrah, it certainly appears that God is a God of fearsome wrath. These portrayals of God have been a stumbling block for many people over the years. I have a friend who struggles to believe the Bible specifically for this reason, because he cannot fathom why a good and all-powerful God would choose to destroy the earth in a flood or rain down fire on a city. If God is so great, couldn't God come up with a better solution to problematic human behavior than destroying entire cities or wiping out all humanity through a flood? Zapping a city with fire (Genesis 19:24-25) and killing off humans and animals through a flood (Genesis 6:7) certainly points to a God who chooses wrath over restoration. So how do we answer my friend? In light of this, we need to shine our Jesus lens on these stories of God's wrath portrayed through the water and fire seen in the days of Noah and the cities of the plain in Sodom and Gomorrah.

UNDERSTANDING THE WRATH OF GOD

Before we tackle these specific passages, it is important to develop a biblical understanding of the wrath of God. Most people believe that God's wrath is expressed through violent actions in which he purposely pours out his judgment on a person or persons because of their sin. With this definition in mind, one would say that the sins of Sodom and Gomorrah or the people in Noah's day were so great that God was compelled to judge and destroy them all. In these cases, God's wrath allowed no mercy toward innocent babies, children, or even guiltless animals. All were killed by God's burning anger.

This understanding of God's wrath gives us cause to ask if God's actions aren't a bit extreme. After all, couldn't an all-powerful and loving God come up with a better plan to redeem people instead of wiping them all off the face of the earth? Our Jesus lens also calls into question God's actions as being rather un-Christlike, as they appear to be actions Jesus would never commit. Jesus died for sinners; he didn't kill them. With these questions in mind, let's once again turn to a Jesus lens to see what the Bible teaches us about God's wrath. We will then be better prepared to take a deep look at the flood and the demise of Sodom and Gomorrah.

As we study the wrath of God, it is important to recognize that the overriding understanding of the Bible is that sin naturally punishes itself.

> Do not be deceived: God cannot be mocked. A man reaps what he sows. Whoever sows to please their flesh, from the flesh will reap destruction; whoever sows to please the Spirit, from the Spirit will reap eternal life. Let us not become weary in doing good, for at the proper time we will reap a harvest if we do not give up. (Galatians 6:7-9)

We reap what we sow. We are punished by our own actions. Sin has this inbuilt energy that boomerangs on the sinner. The psalmist writes:

> Whoever is pregnant with evil
> > conceives trouble and gives birth to disillusionment.
> Whoever digs a hole and scoops it out
> > falls into the pit they have made.
> The trouble they cause recoils on them;
> > their violence comes down on their own heads.
> > (Psalm 7:14-16)

Sinful actions have a ricochet effect on us. In this way the punishment we receive from sin is not so much an act of God that he imposes on us as it is our own doing. Sin itself implodes and punishes us. As Jeremiah says,

> Have you not brought this on yourselves
> > by forsaking the LORD your God? . . .
> Your wickedness will punish you;
> > your backsliding will rebuke you. (Jeremiah 2:17, 19)

Is this not the common reality of our day? How often have we seen this boomerang effect of sin take place in our world or in our own lives?

The New Testament takes this view of sin as self-punishment a little further by associating it with God's wrath. In Romans 1:18 we read, "The wrath of God is being revealed from heaven against all the godlessness and wickedness of people, who suppress the truth by their wickedness."

This verse speaks directly about God's wrath as something that only godless and wicked people experience. Further along in this passage we read that those who are recipients of God's wrath are "without excuse" since God has clearly revealed himself to them in nature (v. 20). Even though God has clearly revealed himself, people have thumbed their noses at God, preferring to let their hearts grow cold to God through their choices to continually sin. The picture that arises from this scenario is that if we constantly go against God, we will slowly reach the point where our hearts have become so hardened that we are no longer able to repent of our ways. We will have reached a point where sin has total mastery of our souls. When this happens, there is only one thing that can turn us back to God, and that one thing is God's wrath. In this way, God's wrath is actually an act of grace, not vengeance, as God isn't into punishing but disciplining those he loves in order to restore them, not destroy them (Hebrews 12:6).

Here is where this Romans 1 passage gets interesting. Verse 24 describes how God's wrath works. "Therefore *God gave them over* in the sinful desires of their hearts." This definition of God's wrath is repeated again in verse 26, which states, "Because of this, *God gave them over* to shameful lusts." And again, in verse 28, "*God gave them over* to a depraved mind."

Three times in a span of five verses we read the words "God gave them over." This shows that the way God works his wrath on those who are without excuse and whose hearts are beyond repentance is by giving them over to their own sinful choices. God's wrath isn't seen in God angrily wiping people out. No, his wrath allows people to have their own way up to the point at which "God gives them over" to their own wishes. The result is that their sins will punish them, not God, and hopefully in their brokenness, they will return to God.

We can see this definition of God's wrath in 1 Corinthians 5:1-5, where we read about a man in the church who was participating in sin. How was this church to deal with the sinner? We read, "*Hand this man over* to Satan for the destruction of the flesh, so that his spirit may be saved on the day of the Lord" (v. 5).

Once again, we read the words "hand this man over," which is very similar to "God gave them over" as found in Romans 1. In this case, the plan was to let the sinner have his way so that Satan would become the instrument of this man's discipline, with the hope that it would result in his spirit being saved.

This theme of handing people over reveals something significant. God, in his mercy and love, plays a role in holding on to us to protect us and influence us to choose righteousness. Unfortunately, there might come a time when our hearts become so hardened by continual sin that we can no longer respond to God. When this happens, God withdraws his hand of protection, he hands us over to our own wishes and allows us to suffer the consequences of our own sinful actions. We see this reflected in the tears of Jesus over the coming destruction of Jerusalem in Matthew 23:37 when he says, "Jerusalem, Jerusalem, you who kill the prophets and stone those sent to you, how often I have longed to gather your children together, as a hen gathers her chicks under her wings, and you were not willing." Greg Boyd writes, "Since Jesus reveals exactly what God is like, his lament makes it clear that God desperately wanted to protect his people, like a hen protects her chicks under her wings. Unfortunately, they were not willing. And since God refuses to coerce people, he had no choice but to withdraw his protection and deliver them over to suffer the death-consequences of their rebellious choices."[1]

With Israel's protector gone, Jerusalem and the temple were destroyed by the Romans in AD 70, just as Jesus had tearfully prophesied. So here we see that God's wrath is not something he does; rather, it is something he relents to as a final option, in hope that the inevitable downfall of those who have sinned will turn them back to God.

The most frightening thing about God's wrath is that he releases sinners, allowing them to go their own way. Without God's protection, sinners are now wide open for demonic attack. The Bible presents the world as being in a state of warfare. Ancient Middle Eastern people envisioned the earth as a primordial battlefield between God and demonic power. God's role in this battle is always as a protector from evil forces that are bent on humanity's destruction. Jesus models this reality of cosmic warfare not only by battling the devil, as seen in his healings and deliverance ministry, but also by describing Satan as "a murderer from the beginning" (John 8:44). John writes, "The reason the Son of God appeared was to destroy the devil's work" (1 John 3:8). A main pillar of the life calling of Jesus was to battle against evil forces. The New Testament continues this theme when the writer of Ephesians states, "For our struggle is not against flesh and blood, but against the rulers, against the authorities, against the powers of this dark world and against the spiritual forces of evil in the heavenly realms. Therefore, put on the full armor of God, so that when the day of evil comes, you may be able to stand your ground" (Ephesians 6:12-13).

Here is the really terrifying thing: If God protects us from being destroyed by Satan and his demonic forces, what happens when God releases us from protection? This is what makes God's wrath so frightening! If sinners want nothing to do with God, why would they choose to wear God's armor? Without God's help, how can anyone stand their ground when the day of evil comes?

With all of this in mind, let's dive into the destruction of Sodom and Gomorrah and the devastation that occurred because of the Noahic flood.

SODOM AND GOMORRAH

Now that we know what God's wrath is, we can get a better understanding of the destruction of Sodom and Gomorrah. When we apply a Jesus lens to our reading of the account of Sodom and Gomorrah, we will be surprised by what we see.

The story starts with three angelic visitors on a mission to check out the conditions of Sodom and Gomorrah. We read that "the outcry against Sodom and Gomorrah is so great and their sin so grievous that I will go down and see if what they have done is as bad as the outcry that has reached me. If not, I will know" (Genesis 18:20-21).

It is important to understand that the text states that there was an outcry to God concerning Sodom and Gomorrah. Did this outcry come from the sinners or from those who were victimized by sinners? Obviously, hard-hearted sinners would not be crying out to God, so this outcry suggests that there were many people who suffered greatly from the sinful actions of the inhabitants of this city. This supports what Ezekiel 16:49 says, "Now this was the sin of your sister Sodom: She and her daughters were *arrogant, overfed and unconcerned*; they did not help the poor and needy."

This all makes sense when you understand Sodom's reputation. Speaking of the Talmud's view of the sin of Sodom, a contemporary rabbi states,

The Talmud imagined that the citizens of Sodom decreed death to anyone who fed the poor:

A certain maiden gave some bread to a poor man, [hiding it] in a pitcher. On the matter becoming known, they daubed her with honey and placed her on the parapet of the wall, and the bees came and consumed her. Thus it is written, (in Genesis 18:20), "The 'outrage' [*za-akah*] of Sodom and Gomorrah is so great, and their sin so grave!" (Babylonian Talmud, *Sanhedrin* 109b)

The Talmud further tells how the people of Sodom offered the appearance, but not the actuality, of hospitality to strangers:

Whenever a pauper happened to come to them, each and every Sodomite would give him a dinar, and before doing so would write his name on [the coin] And, as per a prior agreement, [the Sodomites] would not offer [the pauper] bread. When [the pauper] eventually died of hunger, each and every Sodomite came and took back his coin. (Babylonian Talmud, *Sanhedrin* 109b)[2]

Extra-biblical sources tell us that the inhabitants of Sodom were infamous for their brutality and for oppressing the poor and needy in their midst, as well as for their lack of concern for practicing charity and justice. These sins were anathema within ancient Middle Eastern culture, which held kindness to strangers as a cherished value. To fail to welcome the stranger was a grievous sin. Abraham understood the importance of radical hospitality, as is exemplified in his welcoming of the three strangers (Genesis 18:2-8). Contrast Abraham's actions to that of the inhospitable and murderous citizens of Sodom and Gomorrah. The fact that every male in Sodom wanted to rape these angelic visitors reveals how evil they were (Genesis 19:4-5). In light of this context concerning Sodom and Gomorrah it was very possible that these cities on the plain were cities whose inhabitants were totally depraved in every aspect of their being to the point that their sin had opened the door for demonic activity to control them. Their continual sins had hardened their hearts beyond the ability for them to repent. Now we understand how the outcry against Sodom and Gomorrah was so great, yet sin never goes unpunished. In fact, sin always takes its pound of flesh. This is why we must take holiness seriously. If not, then we fall into deeper darkness that in the end can harden our hearts to the point of no return. When this happens, God has no other choice but to release his hands of protection over us. In this way God's wrath becomes an inevitable reality as God regretfully gives us up to our own doing. In this way the sins of Sodom and Gomorrah turned against them, and the inhospitality that they sowed became the inhospitality they reaped.

When we consider the excessive sin of Sodom, God's wrath as his release of the uncontrite from his protection, and the reality of demonic forces bent on destruction, we can better understand the story of Sodom and Gomorrah. We see that Sodom and Gomorrah had become so corrupted and depraved that God's wrath was revealed by withdrawing his hand of protection over the city, releasing its inhabitants to experience demonic fire reigning down on Sodom. Hosea seems to be alluding to this when he writes, "How can I *give you up*, Ephraim? How can I *hand you over*, Israel? How can I treat you like Admah? How can I make you like Zeboyim?" (Hosea 11:8).

Admah and Zeboyim were cities on the plain and part of the same area as Sodom and Gomorrah that was destroyed. How were they judged? Hosea states that they were given up and handed over. God grievingly withdrew his protective presence by giving them up, and this resulted in handing them over to demonic influences that led to their destruction.

As we apply a Jesus lens to the Sodom story, we can see God's gracious patience in the way that he did all he could so he wouldn't have to hand Sodom over to evil forces. We see this in the way that God delayed his wrath until he sent angels to make a personal visit to see if Sodom's behavior was as bad as the outcry against it. He even allowed Abraham to act as Sodom's spokesperson to bargain with him to spare the city (Genesis 18:23-33). God's grace was evident in his agreement that Sodom be spared if only ten righteous citizens living in the city could be found. Unfortunately, Sodom had only one person whom we know of who was upright, and even his righteousness was questionable, as he seems to be willing to allow his daughters to be raped by the corrupt men in the place of the angels (Genesis 19:8).

According to the text, Sodom and Gomorrah were destroyed by the Lord (Genesis 18:17; 19:24). Two things must be said about God being recognized as the source of the destruction. First off, in the ancient Middle Eastern view, any form of destruction, natural or supernatural, was viewed as coming from a regional god. Therefore, since the writer of Genesis, often considered to be Moses, was a product of his culture and its accompanying worldview, he would have written that the destruction of Sodom and Gomorrah came from God. In a way, Moses would be correct in this assumption, since God, like any sovereign king, would be willing to take on the responsibility for the damage that was wrought on Sodom and Gomorrah by releasing his protection. As the ruler of the universe, whatever happens in his realm takes place only because he allows it to. To use a modern-day term that is familiar to all of us, "The buck stops here, at the boss's desk."

Since God withdrew his protection on Sodom and Gomorrah, he was willing to be recognized as the one responsible for its destruction even though he was not directly involved. God was also accommodating Moses's culturally influenced view by allowing him to portray God in this light. Fire from the sky would certainly appear to Moses as being from God, even if it was actually sent by evil powers.

THE NOAHIC FLOOD

Now let's take a quick look at the destruction that was wrought on the earth through the flood. When we apply what we learned about God's wrath in conjunction with a Jesus lens, we can see God in a different light. The old, more traditional view of the flood describes God as being mad at the way his creation turned out, so he drowns everyone and everything except Noah, his family, and some animals in order to start all over again. I remember hearing a preacher describe God's actions in the flood as taking a big dry eraser and wiping off all the mistakes on the whiteboard of creation so that God could rewrite everything. The problem with this metaphor is that we are not talking about a whiteboard and markers. We are talking about living, breathing people, including innocent children, as well as all sorts of animals and plants.

When applying our Jesus lens to the flood, there are a few things we notice. First of all, we can assume that God waited many years before removing his protection. We read that the sin of the human race was so bad that "every inclination of the thoughts of the human heart was only evil all the time" (Genesis 6:5). For this kind of buildup of sin God must have waited right to the very end, all the way up to the point that sin had fully infected every part of humanity, until everyone, with only one exception, was one hundred percent evil. That one exception was Noah. Yet even after all of this, God still tried to influence fallen humanity to get them to come back to their senses. God called on Noah to build a massive ark in front of everyone. By building a huge ark in the desert, Noah, a preacher of righteousness, would have had many years to warn the people, who would have seen him hard at work, to turn from their wicked ways.[3] As in the case of Sodom, if there were only a few who had repented, God would have spared the corrupted earth from his wrath. As the prophet Joel admonished, "Return to the LORD your God, for he is gracious and compassionate, slow to anger and abounding in love, and he relents from sending calamity" (Joel 2:13).

Sadly, no one repented.

It takes a lot of sin before God will release his protection and thus pour out his wrath. During the Noahic flood, the world was beyond hope.[4] Like Pharaoh of the exodus, people's hearts were fully hardened through their continuing decision to sin.[5] The more they sinned, the harder their hearts became, to the point that they were unable to make any righteous decisions or actions. It is at this breaking point, when sins pile up to the point of no return, that God regretfully releases his protection, and his wrath is experienced.

Once again, we can see how the ancient Middle Eastern view can easily attribute the flood directly to God instead of demonic forces. The author's worldview would lead him to interpret such a powerful action as coming from a regional deity. In the case of this writer, the same writer who recorded the Sodom and Gomorrah account, this regional deity is God Almighty.

But as we have seen in the story of Sodom and Gomorrah, there is so much more happening beneath the surface of the story. As mentioned earlier, many believe that the writer of Genesis was Moses, and in his case he would be retelling a story that took place well before he was born. This would also be the case with the Sodom and Gomorrah account as well, since Moses did not live in the days of Noah or Abraham. Because of this, Moses is retelling what had happened in history, and with that retelling comes an interpretation of God's actions in both stories. Moses would not have had the advantage of applying a Jesus lens to the story of the flood at the time of his writing, simply because Jesus had not come onto the scene by his lifetime. Therefore, Moses would have naturally leaned into the typical ancient Middle Eastern mindset that it had to be God who brought about such destruction.

However, we have an advantage over Moses only because we have Jesus, who revealed to us what the Father is like. This allows us to dig deeper into Moses's writing to see the truth that can be discovered in these stories. Because we take Scripture seriously and believe in its inspiration, we must apply what we know about God as revealed through Jesus to these passages. If we do not utilize our Jesus lens, we will be guilty of not reading these and other similar passages correctly.

QUESTIONS TO DISCUSS

Read Romans 1

1. Were there any "lightbulb" moments that struck you as being very important from this chapter? If yes, why were they important to you?

2. How should an understanding of the boomerang effect of sin influence our decision-making? How do you feel knowing that each sin committed makes the sinner's heart harder, and the more we sin the more our hearts grow cold,

until we reach the point where we can no longer turn
to God?

3. How does an understanding of God's wrath as releasing his
   hands of protection affect how you will live your life? How
   does God's tearful wrath affect the way you view the world
   and other peoples?

4. What are some ways you have seen demonic forces at work
   in this world? What can you do to combat these forces of
   destruction?

5. What is one thing you will do this week in light of what
   you learned from this discussion?

TWELVE

How to Deal with Violence in the Bible

FOR YEARS, I DIDN'T KNOW what to do with the violent depictions of God in the Bible. I struggled to understand how God could order Israel to commit genocide, including killing women and children (1 Samuel 15:3). I also thought that it was a bit extreme for God to bring out a couple of bears to maul forty-two boys, just because Elisha couldn't take a joke (2 Kings 2:23-24). And what about God whacking Ananias and Sapphira for lying (Acts 5:1-11)? Wasn't that a bit much?

The only way I knew to deal with these kinds of passages was to ignore them and try to forget their disturbing portraits of God. I am not the only one who has responded in this way. I know of many other Christians who tend to sweep ugly portraits of God under the carpet. What else can one do with such ugly portrayals of God? This leads us to cherry-pick certain Scriptures we like and ignore ones we don't like. By doing this, are we not in fact truly deciding what we consider inspired and what isn't?

The Bible instructs us, "Do your best to present yourself to God as one approved, a worker who does not need to be ashamed and who correctly handles the word of truth" (2 Timothy 2:15).

Approved workers do not take shortcuts or neglect the hard tasks at hand. Good workers get down to business and work hard on every aspect of their job, including the tough, ugly tasks. To be approved workers in our interpretation of Scripture, we cannot set aside problematic depictions of God just because we don't like what we read, nor can we skip past horrible portrayals of God that contradict everything Jesus represents about what God is like. Instead, we need to get serious about understanding the confusing portions of Scripture that portray God in an ugly light by putting on our Jesus lens and getting to work. With this in mind, let's put on our Jesus lens and examine some disturbing passages of Scripture

ANANIAS AND SAPPHIRA

In Acts 5:1-11 we come across the killing of Ananias and Sapphira. Many flat-text readers believe that God justifiably killed this couple to protect the early church from becoming corrupted by dishonesty. The argument is made that the importance of caring for this upstart church meant that God had to take very drastic measures to protect its health. This included killing off two of its members.

Our Jesus lens begins to shine a cruciform light on this passage to detect if God is being misrepresented as a villain in this story, just as Jesus was falsely viewed as a criminal on the cross. Our Jesus lens also makes us ask, "Would Jesus ever kill someone for lying?" If this is the case, then wouldn't we all be dead by now? Surely, God could have come up with a more Christlike way to protect this church?

It is interesting to note that God is never mentioned as the one who murdered Ananias and Sapphira. In fact, when we do our detective work on the crime scene, we quickly realize that God wasn't visibly at the scene of the crime at all! Only Peter was physically present at the murder scene, and is on record as talking to both murder victims. Right before Ananias dies, Peter asks, "How is it that Satan has so filled your heart?"(Acts 5:3).

Then Ananias dies.

Before Sapphira dies, Peter is on record as saying to her, "The feet of the men who buried your husband are at the door, and they will carry you out also" (v. 9).

Then Sapphira dies.

When you consider the fact that Peter was the only one who was with both victims when they died, he would have to be considered a prime suspect. It is hard to believe that such a highly esteemed church leader as the apostle Peter committed the murder of two of his congregants. If this is the case, why is it that many people believe a loving and perfect God would be the one who killed this couple?

I believe there is a more plausible suspect involved in this murder. Peter mentions Satan as filling Ananias's heart. Could Satan have murdered Ananias and Sapphira? Perhaps this couple was so possessed by evil that it opened them to demonic control and their sinful hearts eventually destroyed them? After all, Jesus described Satan as "a murderer from the beginning, not holding to the truth, for there is no truth in him. When he lies, he speaks his native language, for he is a liar and the father of lies" (John 8:44).

Jesus names Satan as a lying killer and identifies him as the father of lies, which certainly corresponds to the behavior of the murdered couple who were so full of lies themselves.

ELIJAH AND ELISHA

In 2 Kings 1:10-15 we read that Elijah called down fire from heaven twice, killing two companies of fifty soldiers each—one hundred men! What makes matters worse is that these soldiers were, for all intents and purposes, only doing their job as commanded by their king. A flat-text reading would assume that it was God who killed these men. However, when we put on our Jesus lens we are forced to ask if this killing of fifty innocent men is something a Christlike God would undertake. A Jesus lens would also remind us to look back at Luke 9:52-56 to see Jesus' response to his disciples who wanted to call fire down on the Samaritans. The disciples believed God had wiped out the hated Samaritans back in Elijah's day, and they wanted God to do the same in their day. However, Jesus strongly rebukes his disciples for wanting this to happen, clearly revealing that God would never have done such an act. With this in mind it is important to note that Elijah was the instigator, not God. It is clear that this prophet used his divine power given him by God to kill the regiments of soldiers that came to him. It wasn't God who called for fire, it was Elijah.[1] We also see another prophet misuse his prophetic power to kill people. In 2 Kings 2:23-25 we read the strange story of Elisha, who abused his divine-given power as a prophet of God by calling a curse on forty-two boys, who were then mauled by bears.

These stories of abuses of divine power teach us an important lesson. Whenever God gave someone divine authority, he allowed freedom in the way that the person would use it.

The apostle Paul alludes to this when he writes, "The spirits of prophets are subject to the control of prophets" (1 Corinthians 14:32). This is why we should not assume that the way one uses supernatural power is the way it was meant to be used, and we cannot place the abuse of divine power on God for how his people use it.

GENOCIDE

We now come to the horrific passages in the Old Testament that portray God as commanding Israel to commit genocide (Deuteronomy 7:2, 20:16; 1 Samuel 15:3, etc.).

If we read these passages without a Jesus lens, we would have to accept God's involvement in slaughtering entire populations, including women and children, as these modern-day Christian leaders do:

> It's right for God to slaughter women and children anytime he pleases. God gives life and he takes life. Everybody who dies, dies because God wills that they die.[2]

> But one can't neglect that children sin, too. As previously pointed out, today there are kids killing kids, kids thieving, kids raping, and so on. So the innocence of children is a farce.[3]

> Repulsive as it sounds to us today, this ruthless brand of warfare was not technically "genocide" . . . After all, God is the One who gives life. Accordingly, He also has the authority to take it away. His sentence was simply carried out by the agency of His chosen people, Israel.[4]

These are very disturbing words, to say the least, and sound very similar to the way that early colonizers in the Americas used Old Testament passages of God's vengeance to justify killing Indigenous people. In Northern Ireland, Catholics and Protestants have used them to justify violence against each other. As recently as 1994, Hutu preachers encouraged the extermination of their Tutsi neighbors in Rwanda based on portions of the Bible that spoke of God exacting vengeance on Israel's neighboring tribes.

A flat-text reading of passages of a violent God has also provided ample ammunition for the new atheists. It should not surprise us that Richard Dawkins can say, "The God of the Old Testament is arguably the most unpleasant character in all fiction: jealous and proud of it; petty, unjust, unforgiving, control-freak; a vindictive, bloodthirsty, ethnic cleanser; a misogynistic, homophobic, racist, infanticidal, genocidal, filicidal, pestilential, megalomaniacal, sadomasochistic, capriciously malevolent bully."[5]

Dawkins's description of God is hard to argue against if you follow a flat-text reading of the Bible. Yet this description of God is something Dawkins could never say about Jesus, who is God in the flesh! If Dawkins were willing to put on a Jesus lens, his mind could be opened to see that his monster God of the Old Testament is not an accurate depiction of what God is like.

So how do we deal with the conundrum of contradictory depictions of God as one who has no problems with slaughtering women and children, and as the God we see in Jesus who protected women (John 8:3-11) and children (Luke 17:2-3; Mark 10:14-16)?

At this point it is important to note that some Bible scholars believe there is a lack of archaeological evidence showing that the conquest narratives actually occurred.[6] They believe that stories of God commanding Israel to destroy the Canaanites never took place. If this is true, God cannot be accused of being a vengeful warrior God. Before you question if this theory questions the reliability of the Scriptures, it is important to understand the context for why these stories would be in the Old Testament. It was normal for ancient writers to rewrite history to teach important truths and to give hope, courage, and resiliency. Could God have used this culturally accepted style of storytelling as he inspired the ancient Hebrew writers to remind Israel they were children of God, who had not abandoned them? Many of the early church fathers read these passages in a different light. Since they could not accept the violent genocidal God found in these stories they understood these passages as allegories to be applied to our spiritual lives and not as historical realities.

The above theories could be quite a stretch for many readers. I know they were for me when I first heard of them, causing me to adjust the magnification of our Jesus lens by applying accommodation, progressive revelation, a cruciform hermeneutic, and human voice to these violent passages. I looked to see if I could find the enemy-loving, compassionate, Christlike God hidden underneath the ugly images of a violent God. Knowing that Jesus took on the appearance of a criminal on the cross, I had to see if I could find God taking on the appearance of someone he is not in these difficult passages, and sure enough, we can find evidence of this when we reexamine these Scriptures.

Let's start at the very foundation beneath these violent passages.

Then the LORD said to him, "Know for certain that for four hundred years your descendants will be strangers in a country not their own and that they will be enslaved and mistreated there. . . . In the fourth generation your descendants will come back here [the Promised Land], for the sin of the Amorites [a Canaanite people group] has not yet reached its full measure." (Genesis 15:13, 16)

God is speaking of a terrible future in which Israel will be enslaved for four hundred years and then freed to return to their land. While this was happening, the Canaanites would remain in the land until their sin "reached its full measure." It is safe to say that our Christlike God was working his grace for four hundred years on behalf of the Canaanites, but unfortunately the Canaanites chose not to repent, and their hearts grew hardened during this span of grace. Once their sin had reached its fullness, God had to remove his hands of protection and give them over to their own sinful desires.

Before the four hundred years of captivity, Abraham and his descendants shared the land of Canaan with other tribes. However, things changed when Israel left their land and became enslaved by Egypt. Now, four hundred years later, political realities changed. We can see a coming clash of two nations as Israel returns to their land shared by the Canaanites. Great bloodshed was inevitable, as both sides would treat each other as enemies. This was especially the case for the ancient Middle Eastern nations that believed that their gods were warriors who were closely linked to expanding their territories by commanding their followers to take possession of land. Since God allows human free will, he accommodated both the Canaanites' and Israelites' desire to fight over the land, but this didn't mean God was not at work to minimize the damage. It appears that God never intended for any bloodshed to take place when Israel took the Promised Land. In Exodus 23:20-23 we read,

See, I am sending an angel ahead of you to guard you along the way and to bring you to the place I have prepared. Pay attention to him and listen to what he says. Do not rebel against him; he will not forgive your rebellion, since my Name is in him. If you listen carefully to what he says and do all that I say, I will be an enemy to your enemies and will oppose those who oppose you. My angel will go ahead of you and bring you into the land of the Amorites, Hittites, Perizzites, Canaanites, Hivites and Jebusites, and I will wipe them out.

Knowing that Israel was more powerful than the tribal parties living in Canaan, God sent an angel ahead of Israel to clear the path for them to inherit the land. Nowhere in this passage do we read of any form of bloodshed. It does mention the angel wiping out Israel's enemies, but this term "wipe them out" can also be read as "get rid of them" and does not necessarily mean "kill them all." This is further supported by verses 27-31 of the same chapter,

I will send my terror ahead of you and throw into confusion every nation you encounter. I will make all your enemies turn their backs and run. I will send the hornet ahead of you to drive the Hivites, Canaanites and Hittites out of your way. But I will not drive them out in a single year, because the land would become desolate and the wild animals too numerous for you. Little by little I will drive them out before you, until you have increased enough to take possession of the land.

I will establish your borders from the Red Sea to the Mediterranean Sea, and from the desert to the Euphrates River. I will give into your hands the people who live in the land, and you will drive them out before you.

God says that he "will make all your enemies turn their backs and run." This is how God intends for Israel's enemies to be rid (wiped out) from the land. There is no need for bloodshed at all.

At this point in our discussion it is important to realize that it was common practice for people in ancient Middle Eastern civilizations to use exaggeration when it came to warfare language. Speaking of the book of Joshua's conquest narratives, Bible scholars Paul Copan and Matthew Flannagan write, "Joshua is written in accord with the rhetoric and conventions of ancient Near Eastern conquest accounts. Such accounts narrate history in a highly rhetorical, stereotyped, figurative fashion and utilize substantial hyperbole, narrating battles in terms of total annihilation of everyone. To read these accounts as though the author were literally affirming that total extermination had taken place is simply to misread them."[7]

Hyperbolic language is used not only in the conquest texts, but frequently throughout the Bible. Just consider how Jesus says that if your right eye causes you to sin you should tear it out (Matthew 5:29). Or if you have enough faith you can tell a mountain to throw itself into the sea (Mark 11:23). All of these examples demonstrate the need to not take some statements literally, because they involve the exaggerated use of words to make a point.

The use of hyperbole was not just an ancient literary practice as we often use exaggeration today in describing things. I remember when I took my children to see the Harlem Globetrotters take on the hapless Washington Generals. At the end of the game my son looked at me and said, "Man, the Globetrotters absolutely slaughtered the Generals."

Of course, no murder took place during the game. No player was killed, or even hurt. No blood was shed. My son was just using a hyperbolic expression, and I knew exactly what he meant.

In light of the acceptance of violence at this time, God also graciously sends nightmares, terrors, confusion, and "the hornet" (a possible term used to describe reasons to flee) to cause the Canaanites to run instead of fighting to their deaths. This image of the Canaanites being driven out instead of massacred is also seen in Leviticus 18:24-28.[8] In verse 25 it says that "the land vomited out its inhabitants."

We read about the land vomiting out Canaanites again in Deuteronomy 4:27. Does this mean that the land literally spewed out the Canaanites? Of course not. But it does show that God always wanted to use natural means instead of bloody warfare to rescue the Canaanites from inevitable destruction.

In Joshua 2, we come across the opening scenes of what was to become the battle of Jericho. We read, "Then Joshua son of Nun secretly sent two spies from Shittim. 'Go, look over the land,' he said, 'especially Jericho.' So they went and entered the house of a prostitute named Rahab and stayed there. . . . [She] said to them, 'I know that the LORD has given you this land and that a great fear of you has fallen on us, so that all who live in this country are melting in fear because of you'" (Joshua 2:1, 9).

Here we see God's compassion at work as Rahab reveals that her people are melting in fear of the Israelites. The question must be asked, Where did this great fear come from? It appears that the fear came from God as an act of mercy so that they would flee their land without bloodshed.

The world of archaeology has opened the door to reveal more of God's grace. According to archaeologists, the cities that Israel attacked were not highly populated. Most experts believe that these cities might have been small military outposts or populated by the few who refused to flee. But this raises the question, Why did Rahab remain in Jericho instead of fleeing with the rest of the Canaanites? I have a feeling she was not allowed to flee because she was a sex worker forced to remain behind with her family, probably to service the remaining army that stayed in Jericho. So what does God do to her and her family? He saves them from ruin. His mercy reaches out to her through the sending of the two spies who come across her while scouting out Jericho. Now here is the really encouraging thing about God's grace. Consider this question: Why would Joshua send spies ahead of him, if he believed that the Lord had already given them the victory?

In Joshua's mind, the spies were sent as a strategic maneuver, but all along it was an act of God's grace toward Rahab. But there is more. The sign that the spies told Rahab to give the army of Israel also reveals a lot about God's grace.

> Now the men had said to her, "This oath you made us swear will not be binding on us unless, when we enter the land, you have tied this scarlet cord in the window through which you let us down, and unless you have brought your father and mother, your brothers and all your family into your house. If any of them go outside your house into the street, their blood will be on their own heads; we will not be responsible. As for those who are in the house with you, their blood will be on our head if a hand is laid on them. But if you tell what we are doing, we will be released from the oath you made us swear."
>
> "Agreed," she replied. "Let it be as you say."
>
> So she sent them away, and they departed. And she tied the scarlet cord in the window. (Joshua 2:17-21)

I don't think the color of the cord Rahab hung from her window was a coincidence. It was deep red, the color of Jesus' blood. It is as if God is sending a clue hidden in these passages that mistakenly describe him as a warrior God. His grace is peeking out beyond the faulty and macabre portrayal of a violent God.

God's compassion continues right to the end, when Joshua was told by God to march around the city for seven days. Why would God tell Israel to conduct such as unusual battle maneuver? Scholar Preston Sprinkle writes,

> God intentionally has Israel march around the city for seven days. Think about it. Jericho probably contains only a few hundred people (a few thousand at best), and Israel numbers around six hundred thousand! The soldiers in Jericho have seven days to give in to what is clearly an inevitable victory for the Israelites. And yet they choose to reject the God of Israel and defend their city. The point is that the seven-day march around the city could be viewed as another offer of grace by the God of Israel, an offer already taken up by Rahab yet rejected by the rest of Jericho's inhabitants.[9]

In these conquest passages, we can see God accommodating to the ancient Middle Eastern mentality of acceptable violence while working behind the scenes to limit the amount of killing and suffering. Though God is a God of peace, he is willing to be viewed as a mighty warrior in order to keep Israel's trust in him as stronger than the gods of all the other nations surrounding them. Though God is opposed to the bloodshed of warfare he takes on the appearance of a warrior as a starting point. From here, God strives to work with Israel to bring them to a knowledge that he is not a God of violence but a God of grace and restoration.

QUESTIONS TO DISCUSS

Read Acts 5:1-11

1. Were there any "lightbulb" moments that struck you as being very important from this chapter? If yes, why were they important to you?

2. What are some passages you would like to ignore in the Bible? Why are these passages so easy to ignore?

3. What are ways spiritual leaders can fall into the trap of abusing their anointing? Why do people abuse their power? What does this tell you about their relationship with God?

4. If God committed genocide, would he be guilty of abusing his power? Can God abuse his power? Why do you feel this way?

5. Why do some people try to justify the murderous actions of an angry God? What does this tell you about them and their way of thinking?

6. What is one thing you will do this week in light of what you learned from this discussion?

THIRTEEN

The End Times and the Love of God

A PROBLEM PRESENTS ITSELF when we build fear into religion, as it can create a toxic mix that often presents a god who is more like a monster than a loving *Abba* Father. Speaking of the lethal blend of fear and religion, Christopher Hitchens makes his case for supporting atheism. He quotes the following story concerning the way that fearful religion can influence the world in a very negative way.

A week before the events of September 11, 2001, I was on a panel with Dennis Prager, who is one of America's better-known religious broadcasters. He challenged me in public to answer what he called a "straight yes/no question," and I happily agreed. Very well, he said. I was to imagine myself in a strange city as the evening was coming on. Toward me I was to imagine that I saw a large group of men approaching. Now—would I feel safer, or less safe, if I was to learn that they were just coming from a prayer meeting? As the reader will see, this is not a question to which a yes/no answer can be given. But I was able to answer it as if it were not hypothetical. "Just to stay within the letter 'B,' I have actually had that experience in Belfast, Beirut, Bombay, Belgrade, Bethlehem, and Baghdad. In each case I can say absolutely, and can give my reasons, why I would feel immediately threatened if I thought that the group of men approaching me in the dusk were coming from a religious observance."[1]

Religious violence is a regular, ongoing occurrence in our world today, perpetrated by the fearful faithful, and based on toxic images of an angry God.

I find it interesting that the phrase "fear not" and similar words are mentioned hundreds of times in the Bible.[2] Could this be because God knows all too well about our sinful propensity to paint him as a dreadful God? In Jesus, we have the perfect remedy for fear-based religion, as he reveals to us an *Abba* Father God, not a bloody warrior. So how do we understand Scripture passages that seemingly portray Jesus himself as a violent warrior?

UNDERSTANDING END-TIMES PROPHECIES

There is great interest in what some Christians describe as "end times" prophecy. Unfortunately, much of what we have been told concerning the end times falsely portrays God as a violent, blood-avenging warrior.

According to one popular author, in the end times even Jesus himself will be engaged in "the slaughter of millions of people," as "it is the Lord Jesus Christ who crushes out their lives."[3]

In a famous quote reflecting his take on the book of Revelation, pastor Mark Driscoll celebrated the violence and bloodletting in which Jesus will supposedly engage. "In Revelation," Driscoll said, " Jesus is a prize fighter with a tattoo down His leg, a sword in His hand and the commitment to make someone bleed. That is a guy I can worship. I cannot worship the hippie, diaper, halo Christ because I cannot worship a guy I can beat up."[4]

Do these descriptions sound like the Jesus of the Gospels who told us to love our enemies? Are they accurate views of the second coming of Jesus? Does the return of Christ somehow transform him from the Savior who told us to turn the other cheek into a prize fighter with a commitment to make someone bleed? If you read end-times prophecy without a Jesus lens, this is exactly what you get.

A VIOLENT JESUS IN THE BOOK OF REVELATION?

The famous atheist Friedrich Nietzsche said that the book of Revelation is "the most rabid outburst of vindictiveness in all recorded history."[5]

A surface reading of this book would lead me to agree with Nietzsche. As we read Revelation, we are shocked with the amount of violence found in this book. However, when we dig deeper into this book with our Jesus lens on, we begin to see an incredible message of divine love.

The book of Revelation was written by John while he was exiled on the island of Patmos, during the reign of either Nero or Emperor Domitian, both of whom were extreme persecutors who basked in the slaughter of Christians during campaigns of terror. Worried about his brothers and sisters in Christ, John set out to write his apocalyptic letter as an encouragement to the churches in the empire. As a prisoner of Rome, it was important for John to use figurative symbols as code names that his captors would not comprehend. Any letter perceived to be slandering the empire would never have been permitted to leave Patmos.

To understand Revelation properly we must read it in the same way that the early persecuted churches would have understood it. It is also very important to remember that the genre of the book of Revelation is that of apocalyptic literature. This means that John communicated his message through prophetic hyperbole, which was the norm for apocalyptic literature. Without these things in mind, we can easily participate in a gross misinterpretation of Revelation.

As we begin reading Revelation, we must recognize that Jesus is central to the entire book, and is the key interpretative lens to understanding the book. In chapter 4, John describes himself as "in the Spirit" when he finds himself in the throne room of heaven (v. 2). It is here where he later sees a sealed scroll in the right hand of God, who sits on the throne (5:1), yet there is no person worthy to open and read it (v. 3). Upon hearing this, John weeps, but is comforted by an elder, who tells him, "Do not weep! See the Lion of the tribe of Judah, the Root of David, has triumphed. He is able to open the scroll and its seven seals" (v. 5).

The lion can open the scroll, and what does this lion look like?

"Then I saw a Lamb, looking as if it had been slain, standing at the center of the throne" (v. 6).

One would expect to see a ferocious creature that can overpower his enemies with brute strength. However, the lion is really a gentle lamb!

This lamb then takes the scroll, and all heaven worships the lamb.

> You are worthy to take the scroll
>> and to open its seals,
> because you were slain,
>> and with your blood you purchased for God
>> persons from every tribe and language and people
>>> and nation.
> You have made them to be a kingdom and priests to serve
>> our God,
>> and they will reign on the earth. (Revelation 5:9-10)

How does the lion conquer? Through his own blood. Victory has come by way of the victor's death like a lamb. In fact, the image of Jesus as the slaughtered lamb occurs over twenty-eight times in Revelation, starting here in chapter 5, where he is worshiped at the center of the throne of God. Speaking of this, Ronald Sider writes, "Everywhere in Revelation Jesus is the slain lamb. Using this language, Revelation rejects the idea of a militaristic Messiah and explains that the Messiah conquers evil with suffering love."[6]

The image of Jesus as the Lamb of God certainly calls into question what many people expect about Jesus when he returns. Christ comes back as he always was, as a lamb, yet a false image of the second coming of Christ as characterized by a violent display of righteous anger has been preached in many churches. Mark Driscoll isn't the only one who cannot worship "a guy I can beat up." But this belief in an end-times warrior-Messiah dismisses the biblical truth of Jesus as a gentle lamb who conquers through the shedding of his own blood, not through shedding other people's blood. It is interesting to note that any mention of blood in Revelation always refers to Jesus, his followers, innocent people, or nature. Nowhere in the book of Revelation do we see God causing his enemies to bleed, a reality that flies in the face of the claim that Jesus is worthy to be worshiped because he has "the commitment to make someone bleed."

We must allow Jesus to be our interpretive lens in the book of Revelation, for this lamb, not a lion, is the only one worthy enough to open the scroll. And what does this scroll reveal to us about this lamb?

In Revelation 19 we read about Jesus returning and riding a white horse with eyes like blazing fire as he leads the armies of heaven. At first glance, Jesus seems to appear as a ferocious lionlike warrior. "He is dressed in a robe dipped in blood, and his name is the Word of God. . . . Coming out of his mouth is a sharp sword with which to strike down the nations. . . . He treads the winepress of the fury of the wrath of God Almighty" (Revelation 19:13, 15).

A bloody robe, a sword that destroys nations, and a winepress of the fury of the wrath of God Almighty—all very violent images. Yet these images are describing Jesus, who has already been identified as a lamb, not a lion. This image of a lamblike Messiah is crucial in helping us understand how Jesus conquers his foes. Note that the robe dipped in blood is already bloodstained *before* Jesus returns to earth. This is very important, as it can only mean that the bloodied state of Christ's robe is not the result of slaughtering people. Jesus hasn't even entered into battle at this point. The blood on his robe is his own blood, shed for sinners as the Lamb who takes away the sins of the world (John 1:29).

Now let's take a look at his sword that strikes down the nations. This sword comes from the mouth of Jesus, not from his hand. Bible teacher Steve Gregg writes, "Is this not the conquering power of the gospel and the triumph of Christianity? The sword of the Spirit which is the word of God, by preaching, and teaching, and testimony conquers the world for Christ."[7] This sword doesn't destroy people; it saves people as they hear the power and truth of Jesus' words.

Finally, we observe that Jesus will tread on "the winepress of the fury of the wrath of God." We have already discovered the meaning of God's wrath as allowing people's sin to come to its own fruition, resulting in punishment that they have brought upon themselves. In this passage, the sins of humanity have reached the point of no return. God has released his protection over the human race, and now they face destruction as the result of their own sin and their vulnerability to satanic attack. How does Jesus respond to this? He makes wine by treading "the winepress of the fury of the wrath of God." In Jesus' day, wine was always associated with celebrations. In this way, the wine of celebration flows from the conquering Lamb so we can rejoice over all of it. In essence, Jesus is making lemonade out of lemons. Jesus triumphs in the end, and this is great news for the persecuted church.

When John wrote the book of Revelation, he wrote his letter to encourage Christians to stay faithful to Jesus on two fronts. There was physical persecution taking place as the Roman Empire, represented by Babylon in John's narrative, arrested and killed Christians. At the same time, there was a strong emotional enticement taking place through Roman culture, which John describes as a great whore who tries to seduce humanity to follow its ways. John describes the power behind both as evil, satanic forces that pull the political strings in the empire.

In the midst of all of this, John is exhorting the church not to succumb to the empire, because Jesus is Lord and will conquer the enemy as a lamb, not a lion.

Globally, the church today is facing great persecution, and John's letter to the oppressed churches of his day provides encouragement for the present-day suffering church to keep following Jesus. At the same time, it is a wake-up call for churches that are not experiencing persecution. We all live in a demonically influenced empire that seeks to compromise our commitment to following Jesus. As I often remind my friends, "Canada is a great country to live in, but it is still an empire."

VIOLENT END-TIMES WORDS SPOKEN BY JESUS?

Shortly before Jesus was crucified, he taught his disciples that terrible things were about to come their way.[8] In his discourse, Jesus used terrifying images such as the sun darkening, the moon not giving its light, and stars falling from heaven. Many people have mistakenly read these accounts as being literal events that God will bring about as acts of wrath before the return of Christ. Interestingly, these are the very same words that Old Testament prophets used in warning people of coming doom. We see this in Isaiah 13:9-11, when Isaiah prophesies that the sun will be darkened and the moon will cease to shine when the day of the Lord comes. Isaiah repeats this language in 34:1-8, as he prophesies against Edom. Ezekiel uses similar language when he prophesies against Egypt in Ezekiel 30:18; 32:7-8, and we see Amos and Joel using similar words in their prophecies of destruction (Amos 8:9; Joel 2:4-11). Yet in all these cases the sun was never literally darkened, the moon continued to shine, and no stars ever fell to earth. But destruction did come in the form of violence from outside nations.

Jesus quotes Old Testament prophets by borrowing their words to pronounce coming disaster in a similar way to John in Revelation by using hyperbolic language as part of the apocalyptic genre of his day. What he is saying about the sun, moon, and stars was never meant to be taken literally, yet it was meant to be taken seriously, since these words are a warning of catastrophic destruction. Unlike many of us today, the disciples who heard these words understood that the sun would not actually go dark, that the moon would not literally cease to shine, and that stars would not literally fall from the sky. This is because they understood the figurative nature of Jesus' words and their significance concerning the future.

Many people read the words of Jesus in his Olivet Discourse as something that is yet to come that will be accompanied by a great rapture of the saints. However, Jesus himself reveals that what he described in his teachings were to take place in the lifetime of his hearers. In Mark 13:30, Jesus says, "Truly I tell you, this generation will certainly not pass away until all these things have happened." Jesus is stating that the generation of people hearing him speak would experience the events he was prophesying about within their lifetime. Jesus' words were not meant to be understood as prophesying about the very end of times.

So what was Jesus prophesying about? The context of the Olivet Discourse was based on a trip he had taken to the temple with his disciples. "Jesus left the temple and was walking away when his disciples came up to him to call his attention to its buildings. 'Do you see all these things?' he asked. 'Truly I tell you, not one stone here will be left on another; every one will be thrown down'" (Matthew 24:1-2).

Jesus prophesies the destruction that will befall Jerusalem. Sure enough, in AD 70, Jesus' prophecy was fulfilled when the Roman army invaded Jerusalem and destroyed everything in sight, including the temple. At the time of this massacre, the ancient historian Flavius Josephus described the violence:

> As the legions charged in, neither persuasion nor threat could check their impetuosity: passion alone was in command. Crowded together around the entrances many were trampled by their friends, many fell among the still hot and smoking ruins of the colonnades and died as miserably as the defeated. As they neared the Sanctuary they pretended not even to hear Caesar's commands and urged the men in front to throw in more firebrands. The partisans were no longer in a position to help; everywhere was slaughter and flight. Most of the victims were peaceful citizens, weak and unarmed, butchered wherever they were caught. Round the Altar the heaps of corpses grew higher and higher, while down the Sanctuary steps poured a river of blood and the bodies of those killed at the top slithered to the bottom.[9]

No wonder Jesus wept aloud thinking of the future of Jerusalem. "Jerusalem, Jerusalem, you who kill the prophets and stone those sent to you, how often I have longed to gather your children together, as a hen gathers her chicks under her wings, and you were not willing" (Matthew 23:37).

Jesus was very aware of the Jews' desire to violently overthrow the Romans. He also understood the horrible consequences as the result of their violent attempts. This is why Jesus preached that nonviolence was the only way to respond to Rome's oppression. But the people didn't listen, and their day of judgment came about—the Roman army invaded. It felt like the sun was darkened and the moon didn't shine and stars fell from heaven. Through it all, God was not a participant in the bloodshed—disobedient humans were.

With the destruction of Jerusalem came the "end of the age" in which the temple and its priesthood no longer was central in the worship of God through animal sacrifices, the priesthood, and many of the rituals. This was the end of the age Jesus prophesied about, not some end-of-the-world scenario.

WHAT ABOUT THE RAPTURE?

In some circles, God is expected to rapture Christians so that they can escape an angry, vengeful God whose wrath will fall on the earth and those who have been left behind.

What most people don't understand is that what they have been taught concerning the rapture is rather new. In the 1830s, a popular Bible teacher named John Nelson Darby espoused a new end-times theology based on a very literal view of certain Scriptures, to promote a dispensationalist, rapture-based theology that is very prevalent today.[10] What made this once obscure theology so popular?

At the beginning of the twentieth century, Darby's theology found a supporter in Cyrus Scofield, the creator of the *Scofield Reference Bible*, one of the first and most popular study Bibles, who included personal notes in his study Bible that referenced Darby's views. Unfortunately, many who read the Scofield study Bible uncritically took for granted his notes about this fairly new belief, not realizing that what they were reading was something that no Christian would have heard of for the first eighteen hundred years of church history! Influenced by the popularity of the Scofield Reference Bible, many seminaries eventually accepted Darby's beliefs, and graduates from these schools taught Darby's views of the returning Christ as a violent lion. This became the standard belief of many Christians. Yet Jesus is the Prince of Peace, not a god of wrath and vengeance.

THE RAPTURE

As we examine this belief through a Jesus lens, it is important to note that there is no explicit mention of the rapture in Scripture, and none whatsoever in the book of Revelation. The key reference for those who believe in the rapture is found in 1 Thessalonians 4:13-18:

> Brothers and sisters, we do not want you to be uninformed about those who sleep in death, so that you do not grieve like the rest of mankind, who have no hope. For we believe that Jesus died and rose again, and so we believe that God will bring with Jesus those who have fallen asleep in him. According to the Lord's word, we tell you that we who are still alive, who are left until the coming of the Lord, will certainly not precede those who have fallen asleep. For the Lord himself will come down from heaven, with a loud command, with the voice of the archangel and with the trumpet call of God, and the dead in Christ will rise first. After that, we who are still alive and are left will be caught up together with them in the clouds to meet the Lord in the air. And so we will be with the Lord forever. Therefore encourage one another with these words.

Before we dive deep into these verses to discover their meaning it is important to put on our Jesus lens so that, we will see that a belief in a rapture actually opposes Jesus and his desires for his church. This is clearly seen in John 17:15, when Jesus prays to the Father for his disciples: "My prayer is not that you take them out of the world but that you protect them from the evil one."

It is not Jesus' intention to remove us from the mission he has called us to here on earth. We have a job to do, and Jesus wants us to bring his kingdom reign of peace on earth as it is in heaven. To blast us away in a rapture defeats God's calling for our lives, even if remaining on earth involves suffering. Today, as you read these words, many Christians around the world are suffering terrible atrocities, persecution, martyrdom, and discrimination, yet they have not been swept into heaven to deliver them from the misery they face. We all have a calling to fulfill, and suffering is part of our vocation. We only need look at what happened to Jesus' early disciples to see that suffering is part of the lives of those who follow him. They were present when Jesus prayed that they would not be taken out of the world, and his prayer was answered as they faced horrible persecution. Not one of them was rescued by being taken into heaven before their sufferings. Why should we expect anything different?

As we look at Paul's letter to the Thessalonians we must understand the context that Paul was addressing when he wrote this letter. Many Bible scholars think that the believers in Thessalonica faced great persecution, to the point that some of their fellow believers were put to death. Other scholars believe that because the Thessalonians came from pagan backgrounds, they were wondering what happens after death. In either case, Paul writes this letter to give them an answer to their queries about what happens to believers after death. The context of this letter has nothing to do with an end-times theory of a rapture, and everything to do with comforting grieving believers to bring them peace so that they "do not grieve like the rest of mankind, who have no hope" (v. 13), and to help them "encourage one another with these words" (v. 18).

When Paul describes the triumph of God over death, he uses language to which the Thessalonians can easily relate. One of the phrases he uses is "the coming [Greek: *parousia*] of the Lord" (v. 15). In Paul's day the word *parousia* was a political term used to describe an official imperial visit of a coming king to a city. This visit would involve great pomp and celebration.[11] It would also involve a "command" accompanied by a loud "trumpet" (v. 16) to summon dignitaries from the city to come outside the city walls, where they would formally meet with the king to welcome him to their city (v. 17).

Paul is saying that when Christ returns, he will come as a king. There will be a "loud command" and a "trumpet call" (v. 16) that will summon those who have died in Christ to be the first dignitaries to meet the returning king. The interesting thing is that in Paul's day, cemeteries were located along the main road that led to the city gates. So the picture Paul is painting here is a glorious portrait of the return of King Jesus. His readers must have been filled with joy as they read his words and envisioned our wonderful king returning, graves bursting open all around him as the resurrected dead joyfully greet their Savior on his return to earth. What comfort they must have experienced knowing that their loved ones are well and will be resurrected because of King Jesus.

Paul then shares what will happen to those of us who are still alive when Jesus returns. He writes that "we who are still alive" will join our resurrected friends to "meet" with King Jesus "in the air" and be "with the Lord forever" (v. 17). What great news—because of King Jesus, we will join with our loved ones who have died in meeting Jesus. There is no mention of a rapture as an escape hatch from a period of tribulation, and this idea never would have entered Paul's mind.

There is a final and important thing of which we need to be aware. When Paul states that we will "meet the Lord in the air" (v. 17), he is referring to the ancient belief that "the air" was the domain of demons or gods. This is why Satan is identified in Ephesians 2:2 as the "ruler of the kingdom of the air, the spirit who is now at work in those who are disobedient."

Commenting on Paul's words in 1 Thessalonians 4:17, Robert Jamieson, A. R. Fausset, and David Brown describe evil as inhabiting this place known as the "air," over which Jesus will have final victory. They write, "The regions of the air of Satan, and his posse of devils, which now rove about there, watching all opportunities, and taking all advantages to do mischief on earth; these shall then fall like lightning from heaven, and be bound and shut up in the bottomless pit."[12]

This word *air* does not mean heaven, as Darby believed, but a spiritual realm around the earth. This passage has nothing to do with being raptured to a place called heaven so we can escape destruction on earth. What we have here is a declaration that in the end, all believers, past and present, will reign with Jesus over evil. These were comforting words for the Thessalonians, as Paul is telling them that no matter what happens, they will be fine. Why? Because King Jesus is coming back, and when he does, everyone who is in Christ, dead or alive, will reign and rule with Jesus over evil and despair.

Some Christians point to Matthew 24:37-41 as a parable in which Jesus describes a rapture-like occurrence. However, upon closer examination it strengthens the case against a rapture that would take believers away into heaven to escape God's wrath on earth.

Jesus says, "Two men will be in the field; one will be taken and the other left. Two women will be grinding with a hand mill; one will be taken and the other left" (Matthew 24:40-41). The problem with using these verses as support for a rapture is that Jesus clearly states that those who are raptured in these verses are not the righteous, but the unrighteous. He begins this parable by mentioning that in the days of Noah, people were ignorant about what would happen when the flood came and swept them all away (v. 39). The people who were swept away were the sinners. The righteous, Noah and his family, were the ones left behind. Then Jesus links what happened to the unrighteous who were swept away in the flood to what will happen in the future. When you read these verses carefully, you will see that there is no rapture of the righteous at all. It is the unrighteous who are swept away to face God's judgment. This description fits the events of AD 70 when Rome destroyed Jerusalem after the people did not do the righteous thing and listen to Jesus' words of warning.

In Luke 17:34-35, we read a very similar account of this parable, where Jesus describes where the taken person went by saying, "Where there is a dead body, there the vultures will gather" (v. 37). No heavenly rapture here, jut death.

Once again, we see that this relates to Jesus' warning about the death to befall Jerusalem at the hands of the Roman army and is not a reference to a rapture into heaven.

Satan is the one who kills and destroys, not Jesus. Jesus comes to give life.

QUESTIONS TO DISCUSS

Read Revelation 19:11-21

1. Were there any "lightbulb" moments that struck you as being very important from this chapter? If yes, why were they important to you?

2. Do you have a favorite horror story? Why do you like it? Do you think we project our own twisted appreciation of horror stories onto our interpretation of end-times prophecy?

3. What do these two words mean to you: "Fear not"?

4. We all live in an empire. How does a proper understanding of the book of Revelation help you while living in an empire? How does this understanding affect the way we see ourselves, our jobs, our politics, and our world? How does it challenge and comfort you?

5. Can John Nelson Darby's view of the rapture affect how we see our world in the present? Do you think a belief in the rapture as an escape hatch from the earth could influence believers to avoid getting involved in social and environmental action?

6. What is one thing you will do this week in light of what you learned from this discussion?

FOURTEEN

Where Is God's Love in Suffering?

I HAVE SERVED in urban housing projects all my life. In this line of work, I often encounter and experience various kinds of suffering among people I love. Watching injustice, racism, violence, and other kinds of misery takes a toll. Though it is true that every life has its share of suffering, it is intensified in ministry that involves taking on suffering experienced by those one serves and loves. I am sure you would agree. Suffering is an unavoidable cross we must all carry. I often tell my team who serve in tough urban neighborhoods that their job will inevitably turn them into sponges that soak up the pain, the suffering, and the impact of sin in the communities we serve. This is a good thing, because it allows us to help relieve the heavy burdens people carry. However, it can eventually take a toll on us. This is why I do my best to make sure my team regularly rinses out their sponges, allowing Jesus to absorb the pain they carry, because on the cross Jesus soaked up the sins, pains, and sufferings of all humanity. Jesus is the divine sponge who helps us with all the burdens we carry. If we do not rinse out our sponges as a regular spiritual discipline, we will self-destruct emotionally, spiritually, and physically.

I will never forget a specific time in my ministry that scarred me for the rest of my life. Though these incidents happened many years ago, I continue to suffer from the impact they have had in my life. At the time, I was leading an urban ministry that served in low-income, government housing neighborhoods where we ran various programs for children, single moms, and teens. These programs were led by paid staff as well as local youth we hired from the neighborhoods we served. Our goal was to empower the local neighborhood by providing jobs and a leadership development program for urban youth. Many of the teens we hired had participated in our programs as children, and these young leaders were deeply loved by my staff and me. They were amazing young leaders who shone brightly in their communities. One young man in particular shone the brightest. We were so proud of this leader. He was faithful and dependable in everything he did and had a huge influence on many of the neighborhood kids. He was in college, making his mark academically, and his faith was growing and vibrant. He was a terrific inspiration and influence on his family and friends. Yet he was shot and killed by a gang because he was at the wrong place at the wrong time, his innocent life taken away at a very young age. In my grief, I questioned God about his power and love, as I demanded that God be held accountable for letting this wonderful young man die.

A few months later, I was faced with another heart-wrenching tragedy when a young child from our ministry drowned. Once again, I put God in the dock, demanding how a good God could ever let a little child drown. First a murder, and now a drowning. But the catastrophes continued. Shortly after the funeral for this child, I took a three-month sabbatical. I desperately needed to recover from the previous two ordeals and to listen to God. I wanted some answers from God for why these two tragedies had taken place. On the second day of my sabbatical, I broke my neck in a water accident. A murder, a drowning, and now a serious accident, all within a nine-month span of time!

How can a good God allow such terrible things to happen?

How many times have you heard people say things like this? "If God is so good, then why didn't he stop that earthquake that killed so many people?" "If God is so loving, then why does he let people starve to death?" "If God is a God of love, how can a loving God let children get cancer?"

These are all very good questions.

IS GOD IN CONTROL?

Some people believe that since God is sovereign, all-powerful, and all-knowing, everything that takes place in our universe is completely under God's control. If there is an earthquake, God was behind it. Cancer? It's God's sovereign will. World hunger? There is a reason why God is allowing it to take place. To disagree with this view of the sovereignty of God is seen as calling God's power into question. Those who believe this theology believe that anything that happens is intended to bring God glory, even if it's horrific. This is why a pastor told his young daughter that God orchestrated the collapse of a bridge in their city, killing 13 people and injuring 145 others, in order to bring God glory:

We prayed during our family devotions. Talitha (11 years old) and Noël and I prayed earnestly for the families affected by the calamity and for the others in our city. Talitha prayed, "Please don't let anyone blame God for this but give thanks that they were saved." When I sat on her bed and tucked her in and blessed her and sang over her a few minutes ago, I said, "You know, Talitha, that was a good prayer, because when people 'blame' God for something, they are angry with him, and they are saying that he has done something wrong. That's what 'blame' means—accuse somebody of wrongdoing. But you and I know that God did not do anything wrong. God always does what is wise. And you and I know that God could have held up that bridge with one hand." Talitha said, "With his pinky." "Yes," I said, "with his pinky. Which means that God had a purpose for not holding up that bridge, knowing all that would happen, and he is infinitely wise in all that he wills."

Talitha said, "Maybe he let it fall because he wanted all the people of Minneapolis to fear him." "Yes, Talitha," I said, "I am sure that is one of the reasons God let the bridge fall."[1]

I do not question the sincerity of this pastor or his love for God and for his own children. He truly believes that each and every event, even horrible and tragic occurrences, are willed by God to give God glory. How could he not believe this? If God is all-powerful, all-knowing, and completely sovereign over all things, then, in the words of this pastor, "God always does what is wise."

This view of God is that of a micromanager who needs to control everything that takes place. In this view, the entire future is being completely planned and is already settled by God. I call this narrow line sovereignty.

NARROW LINE SOVEREIGNTY

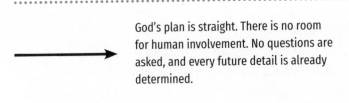

God's plan is straight. There is no room for human involvement. No questions are asked, and every future detail is already determined.

There are two problems with this view: God ceases to be love, and prayer becomes inconsequential.

God ceases to be love

A view that God has ordained people to go through unfathomable suffering paints God as a monster. I know this personally because I used to believe in this narrow view of God's sovereignty. This belief fell apart for me when I went through my personal grieving over the murder of the teen boy, the drowning of a child, and my own tragic accident that I shared about at the beginning of this chapter. How could I believe that a good and loving God could be behind all this suffering, just so he could, in some macabre way, be glorified?

While officiating at the funeral for the young man who was murdered, I overheard a woman telling a friend of the family, "Well, we may not understand it, but the Lord is in control, and it was his will that this happened. Good things will come out of this shooting, and God will be glorified."

Really! God was involved in a murder?

I have heard similar things at funerals for children and others who have died tragically. People often say that it was all the Lord's will, that the Lord is in complete control, and that everything that happens is for the good. But there is nothing good about the death of a child.

Prayer problems

There is another problem we must deal with concerning this belief. If God is a micromanager of every detail and if the future has been completely settled in God's mind since the beginning of time, then why bother praying? Think about that for a while. Let it settle in. If God is totally in control of everything, then why pray? Why pray if what we do or say cannot change the future? Doesn't this let a lot of air out of our prayer balloons? If this is true, would it not be a real downer for our prayer lives? It is hard to be motivated to pray if the future is already fully settled.

It might be a surprise for some that by believing in a micromanaging God, we are inadvertently taking on a fatalistic concept of the universe, similar to that associated with pagan religion, in which everything is set up by the gods and is unchangeable by human action. Prayer has no impact in such a cosmos. Yet the Bible shows us a completely opposite view from that of a preordained universe. In Hebrew prophecy, we read that the future lies in the balance in accordance with human response.

So where do we go from here? There is a second option.

WIDE LINE SOVEREIGNTY

What if God's sovereignty is not a narrow line in which God micromanages every detail and in which everything has already been decided by God? What if God is all-powerful, but not a control freak? What if God's sovereignty is more like wide lines, with open spaces between them, spaces in which humans are allowed to make their own choices and in which spiritual warfare takes place? What if God allows some of the future to be decided by human agency, while also being able to guide us so we don't blow up the world? In this model of God's sovereignty, God is still involved in the world each second of every day to influence us to make right choices and decisions to achieve his good ends. But while doing this, God chooses not to override everything we do.

Wide Line Sovereignty

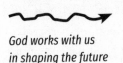

God works with us in shaping the future

God's plan is not straight. It includes lots of human involvement taking place between the lines. The future has multiple possibilities because God has allowed it not to be fully settled. What takes place in the future is affected by decisions that humans make, even as the future is headed in the direction God wills it to go.

In this wide line sovereignty,

God, in grace, grants humans significant freedom to cooperate with or work against God's will for their lives, and he enters into dynamic, give-and-take relationships with us. . . . We respond to God's gracious initiatives, and God responds to our responses . . . and on it goes. God takes risks in this give-and-take relationship, yet he is endlessly resourceful and competent in working toward his ultimate goals. Sometimes, God alone decides how to accomplish these goals. On other occasions, God works with human decisions, adapting his own plans to fit the changing situation. God does not control everything that happens. Rather, he is open to receiving input from his creatures. In loving dialogue, God invites us to participate with him to bring the future into being.[2]

If the future is not totally settled, and free agents, both human and demonic, have a degree of free will allowed within the lines of God's vast sovereignty, then prayer and our responsibility to respond to the love of God make complete sense.

God's love is revealed

The micromanaging, control freak God cannot be a loving God, and this is a problem for those who believe in narrow line sovereignty. The Bible says "God is love" (1 John 4:16). If this is true, then God has to grant us free will. Love will never force people to do what they choose not to do. God has to win us over with his love. In return, God wants us to choose to love him back. For someone to be able to freely love, they must have the ability to make a decision. Therefore, God had to permit free will in the universe.

I'll never forget the day I first met my wife. At the time she didn't know who I was, but I wanted her to fall in love with me. For this to happen, it had to be her decision. I couldn't force her to fall in love with me. If I could have forced her to love me, would that be love? Of course not. It would be evil control.

God is love and he is in love with humanity, and because of this, he can't force us to love him. This means he must give up some of his control, and allow free will to take place in this universe. This means that things will happen on earth that are not God's will or planned by God. If we have free will, then we have freedom to reject God and his ways. We can choose badly and we are free to hurt others. We have free will, so we cannot blame God for the bad that we choose to do.

The same can be said of demonic powers. Because God is love, his love allows free will to be part of our universe. This, in turn, allows for spiritual warfare to take place between the wide lines of God's sovereignty. I have personally participated in exorcisms and have seen, firsthand, demonic powers. The history of humanity is also marked by incredible acts of evil. Genocide, serial killers, violent extremism, and the continuing presence of the many ignorant, evil isms (racism, sexism, etc.), point to the reality of demonic powers influencing the free will of humanity.

Our environment also suffers from human freedom of choice. When sin first entered the world, it affected our environment. Genesis says that because of our sinful choices, "cursed is the ground because of you" (Genesis 3:17). Even today, the choices we make continue to damage our environment. The author of Romans writes, "For the creation was subjected to frustration, not by its own choice, but by the will of the one who subjected it, in hope that the creation itself will be liberated from its bondage to decay and brought into the freedom and glory of the children of God. We know that the whole creation has been groaning as in the pains of childbirth right up to the present time" (Romans 8:20-22).

Natural disasters such as hurricanes, flooding, tsunamis, and earthquakes point to the result of a cursed environment as the result of original sin, as well as the continual rape of our planet through our own sin and greed. We cannot blame God for these things, nor can we blame people who are directly affected by natural disasters, as if disasters were a direct judgment on them from the hands of God.

Sin is also the source of some sicknesses we experience today. Many sicknesses occur because of unwise life choices. Living an unhealthy lifestyle, smoking, overeating, excessive drinking, lack of exercise, constant stress and the like can wreck our bodies. We might also get ill as the result of the pollution we put in the environment or the chemicals we put in our food. However, not all sickness is the direct result of poor life choices. Unfortunately, sickness, even random illnesses, are a present reality as a result of original sin. When sin entered this world, so did sickness and death (Romans 6:23). It is for this reason that we should never blame the victim when sickness comes. This is especially the case when children are ill. Neither can we blame God for illnesses. They are the fruit born from original sin.

Since God has allowed freedom of will, there is a great need for prayer. God wants to give us the joy of working with him in making this world the place he intends it to be. In love, God wants to bless the world through us. He's not agnostically distant, but deeply involved in working with people. God invites us to freely choose to join him in shaping the world. God has things he wants to do, and miracles he wants to perform, but he holds back, waiting on his people to join him in accomplishing these things. We can find out what God wants to do with us by being people of prayer. If there are human or demonic strongholds and powers that could be causing illnesses, injustices, oppression, or any other type of tyranny in people's lives, or in the world in general, then it makes complete sense to get on our knees and battle against "the rulers, against the authorities, against the powers of this dark world and against the spiritual forces of evil in the heavenly realms" (Ephesians 6:12).

However, if God has everything completely decided and under minute control, then why would we need to pray? After all, it wouldn't make a difference, since everything in the future is already settled.

One way of looking at prayer within God's wide lines of sovereignty is seen in the following illustration.

God is all-powerful, which means he owns all the "say-so" there is. But when he decided to populate the creation with free agents, he gave each human various units of "say-so." We each have a certain amount of power to affect what comes to pass by our choices.

Now, because God's central goal in creation was to invite agents to enter into and cultivate a relationship with him, and because relationships are all about communication, God also set aside a vast reservoir of "say-so" that is accessed only by communicating with him. Because of how central this objective is for God, he covenanted with himself to release this "say-so" only if his people pray. There is thus a vast array of possible things that God would like to do but which he will not do—indeed, given his covenant with himself, that he cannot do—unless his people align their hearts with his in prayer. Of course he has the sheer power to do whatever he wants. But given the kind of world he created, there are things he cannot do unless his people align their hearts with him in prayer. . . . This is an analogy that helps me understand all the "if-then" statements attached to prayer in the Bible. It explains the incredible urgency Jesus and the rest of the Bible attaches to prayer.[3]

Prayer and God's sovereignty

God works with us in shaping the future

Prayer is unleashing God's power within the lines of his sovereignty.

This is why James can say, "The prayer of a righteous person is powerful and effective" (James 5:16).

There are some things God wants to do, but in his sovereignty, he has chosen to act in accordance to our prayers. As Watchman Nee said, "What, then, is the prayer ministry of the church? It is God telling the church what He wishes to do so that the church on earth can then pray it out. Such prayer is not asking God to do what we want to do, but asking Him what He wants to do. Our prayers lay the track down which God's power can come. Like a mighty locomotive, his power is irresistible, but it cannot reach us without rails."[4]

BIBLICAL EVIDENCE FOR WIDE LINE SOVEREIGNTY

Does the Bible support this wide line, "room to breathe" view of God's sovereignty? The answer is yes. Here are just a few examples:

> During the reign of King Josiah, the LORD said to me, "Have you seen what faithless Israel has done? She has gone up on every high hill and under every spreading tree and has committed adultery there. I thought that after she had done all this she would return to me but she did not, and her unfaithful sister Judah saw it." . . .
> I myself said,
> "How gladly would I treat you like my children
>   and give you a pleasant land,
>   the most beautiful inheritance of any nation.
> I thought you would call me 'Father'
>   and not turn away from following me.
> But like a woman unfaithful to her husband,
>   so you, Israel, have been unfaithful to me,"
>   declares the LORD. (Jeremiah 3:6-7, 19-20)

In this passage we see that Israel had free will. They could choose to follow God and his ways, but instead they chose to follow idols. In doing so, their future was influenced through their free will. The really interesting thing about this passage is the way that God seems stunned by Israel's decision to abandon him for the false love of idolatry. God seems surprised by Israel's choice to follow idols instead of following him. Twice God says that he thought they would have turned to him. Does this not reveal to us that God has allowed for freedom of choice to take place within his sovereignty? God also seems to have chosen to give up his fore-knowledge within his sovereign plan because he respects human free will. This is why God says "I thought" they would have re-turned to me and "I thought" they would have called me Father.

> This is what the Sovereign LORD showed me: He was pre-paring swarms of locusts after the king's share had been har-vested and just as the late crops were coming up. When they had stripped the land clean, I cried out, "Sovereign LORD, forgive! How can Jacob survive? He is so small!"
>
> So the LORD relented.
>
> "This will not happen," the LORD said.
>
> This is what the Sovereign LORD showed me: The Sovereign LORD was calling for judgment by fire; it dried up the great deep and devoured the land. Then I cried out, "Sovereign LORD, I beg you, stop! How can Jacob survive? He is so small!"
>
> So the LORD relented.
>
> "This will not happen either," the Sovereign LORD said.
> (Amos 7:1-6)

This story is loaded with variables of free will, influenc-ing and shaping responses between God and his people. In this passage God had originally chosen to bless Israel with a great harvest. However, God then chooses to judge Israel and destroy the harvest because of Israel's choice to commit evil. But God changes his mind once again, responding to a faithful man's desires. Amos prays for mercy, and God's response to his prayer influences the future. Amos influenced God to change his mind. In Hebrew, the word *relented*, mentioned two times in this passage, means "changed his mind." Here we see the tug-of-war between humanity and God, each side influencing the other and making decisions that will affect the future.

> I looked for someone among them who would build up the wall and stand before me in the gap on behalf of the land so I would not have to destroy it, but I found no one. So I will pour out my wrath on them and consume them with my fiery anger, bringing down on their own heads all they have done, declares the Sovereign LORD. (Ezekiel 22:30-31)

Here we see God looking for someone to change the course of history from destruction to blessing. This reveals how God has rejected a micromanaging approach to the universe and instead has chosen to work with humanity in influencing the future. Do you see the responsibility we have, and the implications of that responsibility, to follow God by becoming a person who stands in the gap? Do we understand how history could have been different if a person had stepped up to the plate? It is also important to note that in this passage, God's wrath is also affected by human activity. Ezekiel, using apocalyptic language, reveals how God "will pour out my wrath on them and consume them with my fiery anger, bringing down on their own heads all they have done." God's wrath is seen in allowing people freedom to choose evil as their sins boomerang back "on their own heads all they have done."

One way we can look at these verses, as well as many more, is to envision God's wide line sovereignty as follows:

OUR IMPACT ON GOD'S SOVEREIGNTY

God's Will

Jeremiah 3:6-7, 19-20 / Amos 7:1-6 / Ezekiel 22:30-31; other passages—God's plan isn't as controlling and straight as we might think it is, because it involves working with us!

God's Will

Scripture points to God choosing to hand control to us in certain circumstances by granting us free will. As humans, we have the power to make our own decisions, and sometimes we make decisions contrary to God's will, which in turn affect the future. However, God has a response to our decisions. He is able to make a plan B (or even a plan C, or D) to redirect our choices back toward the flow of God's good and perfect will—as is shown by the squiggly lines pointing forward.

We see God working out his good and perfect will despite bad human choices in the following ways:

OUR IMPACT ON GOD'S SOVEREIGNTY WHEN WE DO WRONG

God's Will ➜

- Humankind made some very bad choices before the flood engulfed the earth. But God gave them, but did not force them to accept, every opportunity to repent, and he had a plan B in Noah for the continuation of humanity. (Genesis 6, 9; 2 Peter 2:5)

- Abram made some bad choices in sleeping with Hagar, but God had a plan B ready to help Hagar and also continue the messianic line. (Genesis 16, 17)

- Jacob was a liar and manipulator, throwing a wrench in God's plan for Israel, but God had a plan B in working it out. (Genesis 27, 32)

- David made good choices, but he also made bad choices in his actions with Bathsheba. But God had a plan B to respond to David's bad choices. (2 Samuel 11; Acts 13:22)

- Saul made some bad choices in persecuting Christians, which was not God's will, but God had a plan B for Saul that turned him into an apostle. (Acts 8: 1-3; 9)

- All throughout the Bible, we read of people having the freedom to mess things up with their bad choices, but God is able to respond with a plan A, B, C, and so on.

God's Will ➜

The Bible never says that God micromanaged these people or their choices. But through all the good and bad choices, God was still working out his good and perfect plan through the squiggly lines moving forward.

What a wonderful display of God's omnipotence and love! God can still work out his will while lovingly giving people freedom of choice. God is so powerful that even when we screw up, he has a plan B, C, D, and so on to bring us back on course with his will. It doesn't matter what our past was like or what our present is or even the good and bad choices we make— God continues to relentlessly influence us to make the right choices. God is not a micromanager, he's a composer! He is writing a great musical score called God's Plan. I picture him creating his masterpiece through the stars, trees, birds, oceans, humanity, and to make this more personal, through you. We are all part of God's amazing musical score known as God's Plan. God allows us to be part of his orchestra and choir that get to play and sing his musical masterpiece. Sometimes we're right on key. Other times we're not in tune. Sometimes, we play or sing his song perfectly. Other times we mess up badly, sing off-key, or play a wrong note. But in the end, we are able to look back and discover that somehow, in some way, our magnificent God has created a masterpiece despite the mistakes we might have made.

The arc of the universe moves toward God's good and perfect will as God reigns. "And he who was seated on the throne said, 'Behold, I am making all things new.' Also he said, 'Write this down, for these words are trustworthy and true'" (Revelation 21:5 ESV).

There's a lot in the balance when it comes to God's sovereignty, since God has handed over some of his control to us! In doing so God gives us freedom to choose to work with him, transforming our lives and our world into the kingdom of God versus the kingdom of hell. As choices are made and the future is affected, our good God is "making all things new."

QUESTIONS TO DISCUSS

Read Ezekiel 22:30-31

1. Were there any "lightbulb" moments that struck you as being very important from this chapter? If yes, why were they important to you?

2. How does Jesus act like a sponge in your life, absorbing sin, pain, and suffering?

3. Which belief do you prefer—a God that micromanages or a God that allows freedom? Why do you feel this way? What does a willingness to give freedom tell you about God? What does it tell you about yourself?

4. What does it mean to you to follow a God who gives us free will and allows our actions to have an effect on the future? How does this affect your prayer life? How does it shape your worldview?

5. What is one thing you will do this week in light of what you learned from this discussion?

FIFTEEN

Hell and God's Love

ONE OF THE most frequent questions I am asked is how a loving God could ever send someone to burn forever in hell. For many people, hell points to a God of vengeance and acts as a major stumbling block to ever accept that God is truly loving. However, as we look deeper into this concept of hell we might be surprised by what we find.

The view of hell as a place of judgment goes back a long way. For the first three hundred years of church history, there were six theological schools in the church. Surprisingly, four of these schools taught patristic universalism, while only one taught annihilationism, and the other eternal conscious torment.[1] Though these three views are vastly different in regard to the purpose of hell, they still have a lot in common. All three include a belief that God is set apart above all things as holy. To sin against this holy God is a major offense, and sin must be judged. Where they differ greatly is on the severity and purpose behind the punishment. Let's take a look at how each view expresses their differences.

THREE VIEWS OF HELL

Universal restoration (or patristic universalism)

The most accepted view of hell for the first five hundred years of the church was that of patristic universalism, otherwise known as universal restoration. According to the majority of early Christians, God's judgment for sin is real and also terrible. Sin is a horrible offense against God and cannot be overlooked. However, in their view, a loving God always has a redemptive purpose behind what he does. This means that hell acts as a form of needed discipline used to restore the sinner, not to outright punish the person. In this way, hell has a redeeming, cleansing role to play rather than acting like an eternal torture chamber or crematorium for sinners that has no redemptive purpose. This high view of Christ's complete triumph over sin, death, and the devil left no room for any of God's beloved children to be lost forever. If even one person was to burn in hell forever or be annihilated, then God would have lost the battle against evil. The question that universal restorationists often ask is, "Since God is all powerful and all loving, then why would an all-powerful and all-loving God not save all people?"

Unlike modern views of an easy universalism that preaches all roads lead to heaven, universal restoration teaches that justice will be served for sins committed. There is no "get out of hell free" card. Sinners will still have to face fearsome judgment that involves fire, a symbol of cleansing, before they are fit to enter the gates of heaven. It is through this fire of hell that unrepentant sinners will come to understand the seriousness of their iniquities, and through this painful discipline they will seek forgiveness for their sins by embracing the saving supremacy of

Christ, "even though only as one escaping through the flames" (1 Corinthians 3:15).

Annihilation

Annihilationists believe in conditional immortality. For them, people are not born immortal and are therefore in need of eternal life as a gift from God. Unfortunately, if a sinner dies refusing Jesus' salvific act of grace, the sinner also forfeits his gift of immortality. Thus, that person's mortal soul will cease to exist. Annihilationists teach that hell is seen as a place of complete destruction for unrepentant sinners, who after a time of judgment, cease to exist. Without God sustaining them, sinners will simply disappear.

Annihilationists believe that unrepentant hearts have become so hardened by sin that, even in eternity, they will refuse to repent of their sins. Thus, the most loving and just thing God can do is judge them and then destroy them. A sinner should not endure eternal torture, as it goes beyond the bounds of righteous justice, and takes on the form of grotesque torture in which a perfect and loving God could never participate. As an act of love, God annihilates the unrepentant so that they do not suffer for all eternity.

Eternal conscious torment

The third view of hell is known as eternal conscious torment. This is probably the most common view of hell today, though it wasn't the most accepted view during the first five hundred years of church history.[2] In this view, any sin against God Almighty has everlasting consequences. This is because God is eternally holy. Therefore, any sin against God must be judged as a serious crime that has eternal repercussions. In opposition to annihilationists, those who believe in eternal conscious torment believe in the immortality of the human soul. This is why the unrepentant will suffer for all eternity: simply because their soul is eternal. Eternal conscious torment also teaches that after death, there are no second chances to repent, no annihilation, just eternal suffering in the fires of hell.

Those who hold to the eternal conscious torment view of hell see humanity as infected with sin from birth, thus deserving of God's immediate wrath. For them, God's great act of grace is seen in his patience in choosing not to destroy unregenerate sinners within their lifetime even though he has every right to do so. Those in the eternal conscious torment camp also believe that God's grace is manifested in God's willingness to allow his Son to suffer God's wrath toward sinners who do not deserve to be saved at all.

Each of these views of hell can be backed up with how one reads Scripture. This is why evangelical scholar Steve Gregg can say, "None of these positions can justly be called heretical. All are held by evangelicals who accept the absolute authority of Scripture."[3]

So what gives? How can we have three differing views, backed by loads of Scripture? The answer to this question is that it all comes down to how we interpret the Scriptures.

A good example of how different interpretations come into play is seen when we study the word *hell* in the Bible.

THE WORD *HELL*

Although the word *hell* itself never appears in the Bible, there are basically four words in the Scriptures that have been translated as meaning hell. These words are as follows:

Sheol

When the word *hell* occurs in the Old Testament, it is always a translation of the Hebrew word Sheol, which literally means a place where all the dead, both righteous and unrighteous, go at the end of their lives. It also means grave or the ground.

Tartarus

The Greek word Tartarus is mentioned once, in 2 Peter 2:4, as a prison for fallen angels. When Peter uses this word, it appears that he was adopting a common Greek myth to make his point concerning fallen angels. He does this because his readers would have understood Greek mythology that describes a place called Tartarus where the Titans were sent into punishment.

Hades

The New Testament uses the Greek word Hades eleven times, and its meaning is very similar to the word Sheol in the Old Testament. Like Sheol, Hades was also viewed as a place or abode where all the dead went, both righteous and unrighteous. After the resurrection, Hades will be thrown into the lake of fire, signifying the end of death (Revelation 20:14).

It can be said that these three words translated as hell do not adequately describe any of the three views of hell held by Christians. With this in mind, Gregg states, "Considering the actual meanings of Sheol, Hades, and Tarturas, it seems clear that Christian parlance should never have adopted the English word 'hell' for these terms."[4]

Gehenna

Now we come to the fourth word that has been interpreted as "hell" in the Bible. This word is Gehenna. It is mentioned eleven times in the synoptic gospels, all in words attributed to Jesus. The word appears in only four of Jesus' messages. So the idea that Jesus spoke on hell more than anything else is untrue. Gehenna is also mentioned one more time in the New Testament, by James.

How we translate this word is crucial in shaping the three views of hell that people hold so let's dig deeper into the meaning of this word. The word Gehenna literally means "the Valley of Hinnom" and was an actual place located just outside the old city of Jerusalem that has quite a horrid history. In the Old Testament, it was the place where children were sacrificed to the god Molek by Judah's kings and citizens (2 Chronicles 28:3; 2 Chronicles 33:6; Jeremiah 7:31; 32:35). Later on, Jeremiah prophesied that Jerusalem would be destroyed, and that the destruction would be so bad that this region known as Gehenna would become known as the valley of slaughter, a dumping place for all the dead bodies and rubble that would result from the destruction of the city and the temple (Jeremiah 7:30-34; 19:6; 32:35). Sure enough, in 587 BC, Babylon destroyed Jerusalem and demolished the temple. True to Jeremiah's words, the Valley of Hinnom (Gehenna) was used to dump the corpses and rubble. After Jerusalem was rebuilt, the valley continued to smolder, becoming a garbage dump filled with refuse and worm-infested carcasses. Describing what Gehenna had become, we read that "it was the common sink of the whole city; whither all filth, and all kind of nastiness, met. It was, probably, the common burying-place of the city. . . . 'They shall bury in Tophet (part of Gehenna), until there be no more any place,' Jeremiah 7:32. And there was there also a continual fire, whereby bones, and other filthy things, were consumed, lest they might offend or infect the city."[5]

With this background knowledge of Gehenna in mind, we can understand how various views of hell came about based on it. As a symbol, Gehenna is a poignant representation of hell as a place of judgment, or of complete and utter destruction or a symbol of eternal suffering for those who do not turn from their wicked ways.

In the story of the sheep and the goats (Matthew 25:31-46), Jesus tells a story about a shepherd who separates his sheep from the goats. This shepherd welcomes those he identifies as his sheep into his kingdom because they cared in practical ways for those around them who were in need. These people fed the hungry, gave water to the thirsty, welcomed the lonely, clothed the naked, cared for the sick, and visited the incarcerated. The goats were people rejected by the shepherd because they did not do any acts of kindness toward those who suffered in their midst. Jesus then describes where the goats and sheep end up. "'Depart from me, you who are cursed, into the eternal fire prepared for the devil and his angels. . . . Then they [the goats] will go away to eternal punishment, but the righteous [the sheep] to eternal life" (Matthew 25:41, 46).

Annihilationists see this story as describing the complete destruction of sinners on judgment day. Since they believe that humans are not born immortal, the fire in this passage symbolizes the complete annihilation of the soul as it is burned up. To them, this word *eternal* describes the fire as never-ending, not the soul as eternal. Likewise, the term "eternal punishment" describes the immensity of the punishment, not the length of the suffering. For annihilationists, the soul that faces eternal fire and the everlasting punishment of hell will be eternally and everlastingly destroyed.

According to those who believe in eternal conscious torment, this parable teaches that sinners will suffer forever in the eternal fires of hell. Since proponents of eternal conscious torment believe that all humans are born immortal, the everlasting fire is the place where the everlasting soul will spend eternity. For those who believe in eternal conscious torment "eternal punishment" means exactly what it says. "Eternal punishment" for the immortal soul.

Universal restorationists see these verses in a completely different light from those who hold the other two views of hell. Universal restorationists point out that the Greek word used here for "eternal" is *aionios*, which means "an age or a long period of time of indeterminate duration, or even just a substantial interval."[6] For universal restorationists, "eternal" fire and "eternal" punishment are a misinterpretation, since *aionios* means a period of time that has a beginning and an end. Thus, the punishment of hell would not be eternal, since it is a period of time with a beginning and end.

As for the word *punishment* (Greek: *kolasis*), universal restorationists like to point out that it can be translated as "pruning . . . or obviating the growth of trees or other plants . . . chiefly with the connotation of correction."[7] According to this view, *kolasis* as a punishment has a redemptive quality. It is a form of discipline intended to correct someone, not to torture or kill them.

Given the Greek meaning of these words, universal restorationists make a case that a loving God always has a redemptive purpose in all he does. To them this passage is saying that the goats will have to go through a judgment period (*aionios*) in which they will be corrected/pruned (*kolasis*) before they can enter the heavenly state. On the other hand, both annihilationists and those who believe in eternal conscious torment argue that the period for discipline is an eternal age and that the discipline is destruction or eternal suffering. As you can see, people's view of hell rests on how they understand God, their perception of the mortality or immortality of the soul, and how they interpretate Gehenna, eternity, and punishment.

When it comes to deciding which view of hell you believe in, it is important to go back to the first three hundred years of the early church and learn from the six schools of thought that held different views of hell. Not one of them condemned the other as being heretical. Unlike many today, the church leaders of these schools embraced one another as Christians, no matter where they stood on the topic of hell. Their different views did not divide them. For them, hell was a secondary doctrine that allowed room for disagreement and was not found as a key doctrinal position represented in the Apostles' Creed.

Another view of hell

When we talk about Gehenna as hell it is important to be aware of a timeline for when people will experience Gehenna (hell). Most people believe that Gehenna is a place to be experienced in the future, on the final day of judgment after Christ returns. Yet Jesus appears to speak of "Gehenna" differently. When Jesus taught about Gehenna he spoke in the present tense to warn sinners of impending doom they would experience as the result of their sins. In this way, "Gehenna" was not what takes place after death, but something sinners created now as the result of their sins. All one has to do to see that this is true is to turn on the news and witness the Gehenna we create through our sinful rebellion. It is this view of hell that Jesus' contemporaries would have related to when they heard him speak of Gehenna. This is because they were very aware of how Jesus was saying the same things as the prophet Jeremiah did back in 587 BC. Unfortunately, they refused to listen to Jesus' words to love their enemies, and sure enough, in AD 70 the Roman army invaded Jerusalem and destroyed the temple. As in the prophecy of Jeremiah, there were so many dead bodies because of the Roman slaughter that they dumped them in the Valley of Hinnom known as Gehenna.

HELL IS A KINGDOM IN CONFLICT WITH THE KINGDOM OF GOD

The Bible speaks of hell in a third way. Hell is a kingdom that is active on earth, battling against the kingdom of God. We read, "For he has rescued us from the dominion of darkness and brought us into the kingdom of the Son he loves, in whom we have redemption, the forgiveness of sins" (Colossians 1:13-14).

Two kingdoms, two reigns. A dominion of darkness versus the kingdom of the Son.

What does this kingdom of darkness do? James describes its deceptive power at work in humanity as follows: "The tongue also is a fire, a world of evil among the parts of the body. It corrupts the whole body, sets the whole course of one's life on fire, and is itself set on fire by hell" (James 3:6).

James saw hell as an active force on earth, influencing humanity to do evil. As Brad Jersak explains, "For James hell or gehenna is not a destination at all; it is the source of flames for the accusing tongue and it is the governing power behind the 'world of iniquity.' James is not describing an eschatological oven into which people are cast. Nor is he referring to psychological torments that many now experience."[8]

Jesus saw hell as a kingdom that the church was to defeat in battle when he said, "On this rock I will build my church, and the gates of Hades will not overcome it" (Matthew 16:18).

According to Jesus, a battle is taking place between the kingdom of hell and the kingdom of God. This is why the purpose of Jesus' ministry is described as destroying the work of Satan. "The reason the Son of God appeared was to destroy the devil's work" (1 John 3:8). Jesus calls his church to join him in defeating the works of Satan. According to Jesus, our mission is to storm the gates of hell right here on earth. Jersak writes, "The church—the ekklesia—is a movement that faces and overcomes hades in this world, in this life. Jesus aims the church at the gates of hades, not heavenward. The movement is a downward arrow, from heaven down to hell on earth. What are the gates? Where are the gates? When the church does not know, it has lost its way. But at the foundation of his movement, Christ lays out his purpose: to overcome hades and rescue its prisoners."[9]

CONCLUSION

What do you think of when you hear the word *hell*? Yes, hell can be a horrible condition we find ourselves in. Yes, hell is also an eschatological reality that will take place in the future. But let's never forget that hell is a kingdom that we are called to fight against right here and now. As Jersak rightly declares, "In this model, 'hell' or hades is a kingdom, located wherever people are imprisoned and oppressed by 'the powers' and death-dealers of 'this present darkness'—whether it's the military-industrial-complex, corporate and political beasts, or any personal affliction, addiction or obsession of choice."[10]

These are the gates we as the church are called to destroy. In doing so, our methodology must be based on the life of Jesus. And how did he defeat the works of Satan? Through practical acts of loving the outcast, healing the sick, sticking up for the oppressed, and being a friend to the rejected.

QUESTIONS TO DISCUSS

Read Matthew 16:16-20

1. Were there any "lightbulb" moments that struck you as being very important from this chapter? If yes, why were they important to you?

2. When you hear the word *hell*, what immediately comes to your mind? Why is that image the first thing you think of? What does that tell you about your image of God? What does it tell you about other people's image of God?

3. The word *heretic* has been loosely thrown around in describing people who hold to a different view of hell from others. Why do you think this topic of hell can be so divisive? How can we learn to agree to disagree without demonizing people because of their beliefs?

4. In what way do you see the kingdom of hell as being in conflict with the kingdom of God? How can we defeat the kingdom of hell here on earth now?

5. What is one thing you will do this week in light of what you learned from this discussion?

SIXTEEN

Did God Kill Jesus?

I HAVE OFTEN WONDERED why we call Good Friday "good." Is there really anything good about Good Friday? Now, Easter Sunday, that is good, very good, since it is the day Jesus victoriously rose from the dead. But Good Friday? What was so good about the day when Jesus, an innocent man, was mocked and forced to endure a terrible beating on his way to a horrific crucifixion?

No doubt about it—Good Friday was a horrible, disturbing event in history, the day God incarnate experienced the worst kind of torture anyone could ever go through. But why? Why did Jesus have to endure this brutal and torturous treatment? Death by crucifixion was a horrendous way to die. But Christ's suffering was even worse than the cross alone. He also experienced a prolonged flogging that ripped chunks of his flesh from his body. The whip used on Jesus was a horrible tool designed to inflict maximum pain on a victim's body. Loaded with lead balls and sharp shards, this whip would curl around the victim's body, causing deep bruising while ripping out layers of skin from the back through to the stomach. Jesus was also forced to wear a crown of thorns made to mock him and inflict additional pain as it was pounded into his scalp. The thorns in this crown would have leaked a toxic sap, irritating Jesus' skin and adding to the suffering he experienced. Throughout this abuse, he no doubt felt the emotional pain of abandonment and experienced the verbal onslaught of his tormentors, who delighted in his pain. All of this occurred before he had to carry his own cross, endure having nails driven into his hands and feet, and suffer an agonizingly slow death on a cross.

So let me ask this question again: Why do we call the day when Christ, God incarnate, went through this brutal, horrible, torturous treatment, Good Friday?

The most common answer to this question that many of us have been taught reflects what theologians call the penal substitutionary theory of the atonement. People who hold this view believe that we have all offended God because we are sinners, and as sinners, we deserve the judgment of God for our sin. As one popular pastor who supports this understanding of the atonement has said, "What goes first before the cross is the wrath of God. The only reason you need propitiation is if God's mad at you and will send you to hell."[1]

According to this belief, God is mad at us for our sin and wants to judge us. In this view, Christ took our place on the cross, taking on the judgment of God that we deserved so we could be forgiven. By dying on the cross, Jesus was accepting the death penalty that we deserved so we could be free. This belief is summed up well in a popular worship song that states, "Till on that cross as Jesus died, / the wrath of God was satisfied. / For every sin on him was laid; / here in the death of Christ I live."[2]

Jesus was the substitutionary sacrifice who died in our place to appease God's righteous wrathful judgment for our sin. Case closed. Or is it?

I used to believe this view of why Jesus had to suffer on that horrible Good Friday. I was a firm believer in the penal substitution theory, in which Jesus saves me from God, until I re-examined this belief through a Jesus lens. As I read through the passages that describe the details concerning the passion of Christ leading up to, and including his crucifixion, I began to wonder if this violent view of the atonement was more about us looking at sin and judgment with our own human and fallen eyes. Actions of retribution, torture, payback, and punishment are ideas that we as humans seemingly accept as legitimate forms of justice. Perhaps the popularity of this gruesome penal substitutionary atonement theory is more about us transferring our ideas onto God than about God at all. After all, could these extreme forms of brutalization that Jesus went through really come from a God of love?

When I put on my Jesus lens, I see things differently. With the insight Christ gives me, I can see that the cross was not about appeasing God's anger at all. I now see that the atonement was more about God's love and the lengths to which God will go to bring forgiveness and grace to sinners like me. Jesus even forgives us from the cross! With a Jesus lens, I can see that Jesus came to show us how different God is from the way that we perceive him. I began to realize that the greatest revelation of God's supremacy and power is seen not in his judgment and wrath, but in his love as seen on the cross where God willingly suffered at the hands of sinners.

When I think of the crucifixion and all that led up to it, I can understand why Jesus was willing to be tortured in our place to pay the price for our sins and to free us from impending judgment. This depth of loving sacrifice is in the very nature of Christ, and it is no surprise that Jesus would go to these lengths to save us sinners. However, upon closer examination, my Jesus lens cannot reconcile with an image of a vengeful God demanding his pound of flesh with vehement fury. Beatings, mocking, whipping, nails, torture. I cannot see God participating in the over-the-top violence that took place on Good Friday.

The un-Christlike God of the penal substitutionary atonement has more in common with the ancient Middle Eastern god Molek, whose wrath could be appeased only through child sacrifice. Is God just like this despicable pagan god? Of course not. We have a Christlike God who, unlike Molek and other pagan deities, came in the flesh to show us how much we are loved by our heavenly Father. It is unfathomable that our Christlike God could ever participate in the child sacrifice and torture of his own Son. God is not Molek. He doesn't delight in human sacrifices. For God to participate in such evil would mean that he would have to directly disobey his own commandment against human and child sacrifices (see Leviticus 18:21; 20:3; Deuteronomy 12:31; 18:10; 2 Kings 21:6).

A Jesus lens also leads us to ask about Jesus' commandments to love our enemies and to pray for those who persecute us. Jesus said that if we do these things, we will be children of our Father in heaven (Matthew 5:44-48). God loves it when his children act like him—loving, caring, and forgiving our enemies. If this is true, shouldn't these commandments to love our enemies also apply to God the Father? And what about God's commandment not to kill (Exodus 20:13)? Wouldn't God, in taking Jesus' life, be guilty of breaking one of his own Ten Commandments? First Corinthians 13:5 tells us that love keeps no record of wrongs. If this is the case, then how can God, whom the Bible describes as love, hold so tightly to our record of wrongs that he would take it out on his Son (1 John 4:8, 16)?

Finally, I was left with this question: Why does God have to be paid off before he can forgive us? Isn't forgiveness something that is offered unconditionally? To forgive someone is an act that the offended person chooses, without demanding anything in return. Given this, the penal substitutionary view of the atonement is not about true forgiveness. It's a payoff in order to get forgiveness which isn't really forgiveness at all.

Thinking through these questions raised by reading Scripture through my Jesus lens caused me to seek another pathway to truth. These questions allowed me to venture off the well-trodden hiking trail to find another possible reason for why Jesus had to go through this brutal, horrible, and torturous treatment. This side trail led me to the early church. I discovered that the early church fathers did not see an angry, retributive God as the centerpiece of the crucifixion. In fact, their view was the complete opposite. The idea that God had to be paid off so that sinners could receive salvation was the furthest thing from their minds.[3] To them, the blood, guts, and gore that Jesus went through were not caused by God and his angry judgment. Instead, the suffering Jesus endured was the activity of Satan and fallen humanity. It was sin, not God, that put Jesus on the cross. And it was disobedient sinners and demonic influences who tortured Christ, nailed him to the cross, and crucified Jesus—not God! And while Jesus took the sins of the world upon himself on that dirty cross it was in his death that he destroyed them all. As Jesus rose victorious over the grave, sin, death, and the devil were defeated.

The early church called this view of salvation *Christus Victor* (Christ the Victor).[4] In this view, the cross was not Godward in its need to appease God. On the contrary, the cross was Satanward in its defeat of the evil powers that held humanity in bondage. For these ancient Christians, Jesus was on a quest to destroy evil and restore everything that evil destroyed. Jesus' entire life, death, and resurrection were all about establishing the kingdom of God in opposition to the kingdom of darkness.[5] Each exorcism, every healing, and the many confrontations with the powers that be were all expressions of Jesus' mission to "destroy the devil's work" (1 John 3:8). The cross was the final masterpiece and icing on the cake, revealing that sin, death, and the devil were no match for God's loving forgiveness. A Christus Victor view of the cross proclaims that Jesus didn't come to save us from our sins by appeasing an angry God. Instead, a Christus Victor view triumphantly declares that Jesus has won us complete victory over the devastating powers of sin, death, and the devil, through his life, death, and resurrection. In Christus Victor, Jesus accomplishes much more than just alleviating our guilt for sin. A Christus Victor view declares that Jesus destroyed evil and is restoring everything ruined by evil.

The penal substitutionary and Christus Victor views of the atonement each hold a different understanding of what God is like. Those who support the penal substitutionary theory have a view of God as angry. In their view, God's law has been broken by sin, and this makes God angry at us. Since we have offended a holy God through our lawlessness, we deserve to be severely punished for breaking God's rules. However, those who hold to a Christus Victor view see God in an eternally loving way. Those who believe in the Christus Victor view do not see the atonement through legal eyes, as justly deserved punishment, but more through medical eyes, as healing. This certainly fits with what Jesus said about his ministry. "It is not the healthy who need a doctor, but the sick. I have not come to call the righteous, but sinners" (Mark 2:17).

This Christus Victor view of the atonement as a cure for sin is described well by Brad Jersak when he says, "When has fear or anger ever cured a disease? When has shame and guilt ever restored someone's life? When has punishing the victim ever transformed a heart or life? So it is with sin. As a disease, it cannot be punished out of us! We don't need a punishing Judge, but rather, a great Physician."[6]

Jesus' life gave testimony to warfare against the kingdom of darkness. As mentioned earlier, his miracles, healings, and exorcisms were all signs that through his kingdom reign, he had come to defeat Satan's kingdom of darkness, which had enveloped the earth. This warfare led Jesus to the cross for the ultimate showdown with the devil.

Before his arrest, Jesus said "'Now is the time for judgment on this world; now the prince of this world will be driven out. And I, when I am lifted up from the earth, will draw all people to myself.' He said this to show the kind of death he was going to die" (John 12:31-33).

The apostle John sums up the life of Jesus by reminding us that "the reason the Son of God appeared was to destroy the devil's work" (1 John 3:8).

The writer of Hebrews states that Jesus frees us from the power of sin, death, and the devil. "Since the children have flesh and blood, he too shared in their humanity so that by his death he might break the power of him who holds the power of death—that is, the devil—and free those who all their lives were held in slavery by their fear of death" (Hebrews 2:14-15).

This idea of Jesus rescuing us from the power of Satan is also seen in Colossians 1:13-14, where we read this about God: "For he has rescued us from the dominion of darkness and brought us into the kingdom of the Son he loves, in whom we have redemption, the forgiveness of sins."

This wonderful Christus Victor message was what the first church in the book of Acts preached. None of the sermons in Acts state that the death of Christ was about appeasing God's wrath. However, they do speak clearly about the victorious Jesus as Lord over all. The message of the early church was a simple invitation for people to repent and turn to Jesus as Lord. In Acts, sin, death, and the devil have been defeated by the risen Christ.

When we consider Good Friday through a Jesus lens, it becomes clear that the purpose of Jesus' death wasn't to rescue us from the violence of God. Far from it. Good Friday was about rescuing us from the power of Satan. It was always this way. In his life, death, and resurrection, Christ was continually delivering us from the power of Satan. This deliverance culminated in Satan and his willing co-conspirators, sinful humans like you and me, yelling "Crucify him!" God wasn't torturing Jesus. Roman soldiers, representing the powers that be, were the ones who took great delight in brutalizing Jesus. Satan, sin, and humanity were the ones who put Jesus on that cross, not God.

THE CROSS AS THE ULTIMATE SIGN OF GOD'S LOVE

Theologians have rightly stated that the cross is the most definitive sign of what God is like. As Brian Zahnd states, "At the cross Jesus does not save us from God; at the cross Jesus reveals God as savior! When we look at the cross we don't see what God does; we do see who God is!"[7]

The cross exposes our sin and reveals the ugliness of the kingdom of darkness all around us. Yet at the same time, it acts as a great symbol, reflecting how much God loves us. The extreme suffering of Christ on the cross is a visual of God's extreme love for sinners. After all, what type of being would be willing to suffer the way Jesus did on the cross? Why would anyone in their right mind willingly choose to go through what Jesus endured?

"Greater love has no one than this: to lay down one's life for one's friends" (John 15:13).

The cross reveals the immense, eternal, and unstoppable love that God has for fallen humanity. Only this kind of love would allow a beloved Son to be crucified, and only this type of love can respond to such barbaric hate by saying, "Father, forgive them" (Luke 23:34).

In trying to describe the love of Jesus, the great mystic Saint John of the Cross wrote this beautiful poem.

A lone young shepherd lived in pain
Withdrawn from pleasure and contentment,
His thoughts fixed on a shepherd-girl
His heart an open wound of love.

He weeps, but not from the wound of love,
There is no pain in such a wound
However deeply it wounds the heart;
He weeps in knowing he's been forgotten.

That one thought: his shining one
Has forgotten him, is such great pain
That he gives himself up to brutal handling in a foreign land,
His heart an open wound with love.

The shepherd says: I pity the one
Who draws himself back from my love,
And does not seek the joy of my presence,
Though my heart is an open wound with love for him.

After a long time he climbed a tree,
And spread his shining arms,
And hung by them, and died,
His heart an open wound of love.

So let me ask this question: Why did Christ go through all of this brutal, horrible torturous treatment? The answer to the reason Jesus suffered so much agony is because of love—Christ's extreme love for you and me drove him to embrace the suffering that he endured. Christ's act of extreme love by accepting the horrible beating and crucifixion was for all of us. He went through this torturous process to ransom us from sin, death, and the devil. How does one respond to a love like this? It's simple—choose to love Jesus back.

In John 1:12 we read, "Yet to all who did receive him, to those who believed in his name, he gave the right to become children of God."

Because of his great love, Jesus has opened the door for all of us to become children of God. All we need to do is say yes to Christ's love. This is what it means to receive him. Just say yes to Jesus. Say yes to his love. Say yes to his sacrifice as a ransom to set us free. Say yes to his victory over Satan, death, and sin. Just say yes to Jesus.

QUESTIONS TO DISCUSS

Read Matthew 27:22-56

1. Were there any "lightbulb" moments that struck you as being very important from this chapter? If yes, why were they important to you?

2. Do you think Good Friday is "good?" Why do you feel this way?

3. What does the willingness of Jesus to suffer so much pain and shame tell you about Jesus the Son? What does it tell you about God the Father?

4. In what ways does Jesus dying and being raised from the dead defeat sin, death, and the devil? How can we live in this freedom of Christus Victor?

5. Have you said yes to Jesus? If not, what's holding you back?

6. What is one thing you will do this week in light of what you learned from this discussion?

A Final Word

From Deconstruction to Reconstruction

I HOPE YOU have been challenged, encouraged, or maybe even upset by what you read in this book. Each one of these reactions means that there is some movement taking place in the depths of your soul. But what now? What do you do with everything that has been stirred up inside you after reading this book?

A wise man once said,

> Do not merely listen to the word, and so deceive yourselves. Do what it says. Anyone who listens to the word but does not do what it says is like someone who looks at his face in a mirror and, after looking at himself, goes away and immediately forgets what he looks like. But whoever looks intently into the perfect law that gives freedom, and continues in it—not forgetting what they have heard, but doing it—they will be blessed in what they do. (James 1:22-25)

This book is full of Scripture. Now it is up to you to apply what you read. Don't put this book down and walk away, immediately forgetting what God has told you while you were reading. Write out an action plan so you can live what you learned. Spend time in prayer. Journal what your heart has said to you. Share what you have learned with others. Blog your thoughts to the world. Create a book club to discuss this book. Do something, anything, so you don't forget what God has said to you while you were reading this book. Whatever you do, "do not merely listen to the word, and so deceive yourselves. Do what it says" (James 1:22).

For some of you, this book has launched you into the journey of faith deconstruction. For others, you might already be a long way on your journey of deconstruction, while some of you might be seeking to learn more about Christianity. No matter where you are at, I hope you make Jesus central to guide you on your adventure. I also hope you find yourself a haverim and use this book as a trusted tool with which to have sacred arguments along the way.

Recently, a friend of mine shared these words with me concerning his journey of deconstruction: "If I talk to anyone, they think I'm a heretic, crazy, or they just don't know how to respond. So, now I don't say anything."

Going through deconstruction can be a frightening journey. It isn't easy facing your doubts and challenging the beliefs that you once held dear. Like my friend, you may often feel alone. Have hope. The good news is that there is a great blessing awaiting you at the end of the tunnel.

As I look back over my times of deconstruction, I have always benefited greatly because of it. Each question, every doubt, and the various struggles that come my way and challenge my faith are steps forward that my *Abba* can use to bring me closer to him.

As Saint John of the Cross wrote, "To reach union with the wisdom of God, a person must advance by unknowing rather than by knowing."[1]

To experience a depth in our union of God, we need to trust the process of unknowing everything we thought we knew.

God frees me from the chains of what I thought were certainties when I embrace a humility of unknowing. By looking to Jesus, "the author and finisher of my faith" (Hebrews 12:2 KJV), I have grown in my love for Scripture accompanied by a deeper sense of peace and joy as I grow closer to my loving *Abba*.

None of this should surprise us. After all, Jesus told us, "I am the way and the truth and the life. No one comes to the Father except through me" (John 14:6).

When we make Jesus central to all we do and truly follow him, he will take us to the Father of love. And it is here where we truly experience, as John 10:10 attests, life to the full.

Next Steps

Keep the Conversation Going

DO YOU HAVE QUESTIONS, thoughts, or ideas? Are you in need of some assistance to help you along the way? Please feel free to check out various resources and opportunities available to you at www.connectcity.org/letthelightin to help you on your journey with Jesus.

Acknowledgments

I WANT TO THANK my beautiful wife, who patiently supported me throughout the writing of this book. Love you, Jude. I also want to acknowledge my children, who as young adults keep me on my toes by staying in touch with our ever-changing culture. A special shout-out to my Connect City team. It is an honor to work alongside you all as we join Jesus in what he is doing all around us. Finally, I want to acknowledge my dear old Mom. As she nears the end of her earthly journey I am indebted to her for giving me that Irish stubbornness to never hide from the truth that sets us all free!

Notes

INTRODUCTION

1 "Being confident of this, that he who began a good work in you will carry it on to completion until the day of Christ Jesus" (Philippians 1:6).

2 "For no one can lay any foundation other than the one already laid, which is Jesus Christ. If anyone builds on this foundation using gold, silver, costly stones, wood, hay or straw, their work will be shown for what it is, because the Day will bring it to light. It will be revealed with fire, and the fire will test the quality of each person's work. If what has been built survives, the builder will receive a reward. If it is burned up, the builder will suffer loss but yet will be saved—even though only as one escaping through the flames" (1 Corinthians 3:11-15).

3 I appeal to Saint John of the Cross as an expert concerning matters of the soul. As one who suffered greatly because of his love for Christ and the poor, accompanied by his deep biblical knowledge and skill as a spiritual director, Father John has much to teach us about the Spirit's activity of renewal in our innermost being.

4 Saint John of the Cross actually never used the phrase "dark night of the soul"; instead he chose to use the phrase "dark night of the senses and dark night of the spirit" to describe what happens in the souls of those who go through this process of deconstruction. I have chosen to use the familiar phrase "dark night of the soul," which has frequently been attributed to him, as a summary statement that includes darkness of senses and spirit.

5 I share the story of these tragedies and what I learned from them in my book *The Beautiful Disappointment: Discovering Who You Are through the Trials of Life* (Castle Quay Books, 2008).

6 *The Collected Works of St. Teresa of Ávila*, Kieran Kavanaugh and Otilio Rodriguez, trans., vol. 1 (Washington, DC: ICS Publications, 1987), 113.

7 Kieran Kavanaugh, ed., *John of the Cross: Selected Writings* (New York: Paulist Press, 1987), 59.

8 Ibid.

9 "No one sews a patch of unshrunk cloth on an old garment, for the patch will pull away from the garment, making the tear worse. Neither do people pour new wine into old wineskins. If they do, the skins will burst; the wine will run out and the wineskins will be ruined. No, they pour new wine into new wineskins, and both are preserved" (Matthew 9:16-17).

10 "Now the Berean Jews were of more noble character than those in Thessalonica, for they received the message with great eagerness and examined the Scriptures every day to see if what Paul said was true" (Acts 17:11).

11 Jesus refers to his reign in the cosmos as the kingdom of God.

12 All one has to do is read church history to see the shocking ways the church silenced people by killing them and justifying it in the name of heresy. Today, the religious establishment cannot kill people, but they can brandish the word *heretic* to silence people.

13 "As a man he struggled with God. / He struggled with the angel and overcame him; / he wept and begged for his favor. / He found him at Bethel / and talked with him there— / the LORD God Almighty, / the LORD is his name!" (Hosea 12:3-5).

14 "Continue to work out your salvation with fear and trembling" (Philippians 2:12).

PART ONE EPIGRAPH

Quoted in Stoyan Zaimov, "Eugene Peterson's Son Reveals His Father 'Fooled' Everyone, Had Only One Real Sermon for the World," *Christian Post*, November 5, 2018, https://www.christianpost.com/news/eugene -petersons-son-reveals-his-father-fooled-everyone-had-only-one-real-sermon -for-the-world.html.

CHAPTER 1

1 You can read various free downloads of this message online. The Monergism website includes a version at https://www.monergism.com/ thethreshold/sdg/pdf/edwards_angry.pdf.

2 Jonathan Edwards, "Sinners in the Hands of an Angry God" (sermon, Enfield, MA [now CT], July 8, 1741).

3 John Piper, "God Loves the Sinner, but Hates the Sin?," episode 140, July 30, 2013, in *Ask Pastor John*, podcast, MP3 audio, https://www .desiringgod.org/interviews/god-loves-the-sinner-but-hates-the-sin.

4 Ibid.

5 I find it very disturbing that this Bible teacher even misquotes John 3:16 to make his point by stating, "For God so loved the world that he hates . . ." However, John 3:16 states: "For God so loved the world that he gave his one and only Son, that whoever believes in him shall not perish but have eternal

life." There is nothing in John 3:16 that states that God hates us, but quite the contrary. He loves us so much that he gave his one and only Son to save us. That's not an act of hate, its an act of incredible love. And let us not forget the next verse, "For God did not send his Son into the world to condemn the world, but to save the world through him" (v. 17). Once again there is no mention of God's wrath, no intentions for punishment, not even a desire for condemnation. God's loving purpose is to save, not condemn.

6 Andrew Newberg and Mark Robert Waldman, *How God Changes Your Brain: Breakthrough Findings from a Leading Neuroscientist* (New York: Ballentine Books, 2009), 107.

7 The new atheists is a label given to a movement of modern-day atheists who are aggressively active in standing against any forms of faith and its influence on society, especially with young people. Some people have called this movement fundamentalist or militant atheism.

8 This is called the penal substitution theory of the atonement, and I will address this issue later on in the book.

9 We will get more into this in chapter 16, "Did God Kill Jesus?"

CHAPTER 2

1 A. W. Tozer, *The Knowledge of the Holy: The Attributes of God: Their Meaning in the Christian Life* (New York: HarperCollins, 1978), 1.

2 Speaking of Jesus, Matthew 3:12 reads, "His winnowing fork is in his hand, and he will clear his threshing floor, gathering his wheat into the barn and burning up the chaff with unquenchable fire."

3 Timothy R. Jennings, *The God-Shaped Brain: How Changing Your View of God Transforms Your Life* (Downers Grove: IVP, 2017), 27.

4 See the story of the prodigal son in Luke 15:11-32.

5 *Guardians of the Flame*, directed by Joshua Eaves (Rostrevor, NIR: Global Fire Creative, 2018), https://www.guardiansoftheflame.org/the-documentary.

6 Judith and Colin McCarthy, *What Does Justice Look Like and Why Does God Care about It?* (Harrisonburg, VA: Herald Press, 2020), 59–60. To learn more about this wonderful ministry, visit Casa Rocha's website at www .jocumcasarocha.com.br.

CHAPTER 3

1 Paul tells us to "be transformed by the renewing of your mind" (Romans 12:2).

2 These leaders often misquote Habakkuk 1:13, which says, "Your eyes are too pure to look on evil; you cannot tolerate wrongdoing." It is important to note that in this verse, the prophet Habakkuk is making this claim about God, so these are not the words of God about himself. In fact, if we read further in this chapter, we see how God indeed tolerates wickedness.

3 This story is from my friend Tony Campolo. To read the story in its entirety, see "Don't Despise the Small Things," *End Slavery Tennessee* (blog),

July 18, 2009, https://www.endslaverytn.org/blog/dont-despise-the-small
-things.

4 No one knows for sure where this quote came from. Some people accredit
it to Voltaire or Mark Twain or someone else. Regardless, it is a great description of what we do to God.

5 I doubt that I came up with this metaphor myself. It must have come from
someone else that I might have heard or read. If this is the case, I apologize
for not remembering the reference for this.

6 Richard Rohr, "Love, Not Atonement," Center for Action and Contemplation, May 4, 2017, https://cac.org/love-not-atonement-2017-05-04/.

CHAPTER 4

1 We see God's great desire for mercy in Micah 6:8, where we read, "He has
shown you, O mortal, what is good. / And what does the LORD require of
you? / To act justly and to love mercy / and to walk humbly with your God."
Jesus echoes this verse in his many interactions with religious elites who completely misunderstand the heart of God, as seen in this story of the prodigal
son and elsewhere throughout the Gospels, including in Matthew 9:10-13:
"While Jesus was having dinner at Matthew's house, many tax collectors and
sinners came and ate with him and his disciples. When the Pharisees saw this,
they asked his disciples, 'Why does your teacher eat with tax collectors and
sinners?' On hearing this, Jesus said, 'It is not the healthy who need a doctor,
but the sick. But go and learn what this means: 'I desire mercy, not sacrifice.'
For I have not come to call the righteous, but sinners.'"

2 Brennan Manning, *Abba's Child: The Cry of the Heart for Intimate Belong-
ing* (Colorado Springs: NavPress, 2002), 19–20.

3 We will talk more about God's wrath, as seen in God's letting us go our
own way, in chapter 11.

4 My friend is Tony Campolo.

5 See Colossians 1:18.

PART TWO EPIGRAPH

Brian Zahnd, *Sinners in the Hands of a Loving God: The Scandalous Truth of
the Very Good News* (New York: Waterbrook, 2017).

CHAPTER 5

1 For example, "Slaves, obey your earthly masters with respect and fear, and
with sincerity of heart, just as you would obey Christ. Obey them not only
to win their favor when their eye is on you, but as slaves of Christ, doing the
will of God from your heart. Serve wholeheartedly, as if you were serving the
Lord, not people, because you know that the Lord will reward each one for
whatever good they do, whether they are slave or free" (Ephesians 6:5-8).

2 Noel Rae, "How Christian Slaveholders Used the Bible to Justify Slavery,"
Time, February 23, 2018, https://time.com/5171819/christianity-slavery

-book-excerpt/. Adapted from Noel Rae, *The Great Stain: Witnessing American Slavery* (New York: Overlook Press, 2018).

3 See Deuteronomy 7:1-2; 20:16-17.

4 Quoted in Brian Zahnd, *Sinners in the Hands of a Loving God: The Scandalous Truth of the Very Good News* (New York: Waterbrook, 2017), 33.

5 Quoted in ibid., 34

6 John Piper, "What Made It Okay for God to Kill Women and Children in the Old Testament?," Desiring God, February 27, 2010, YouTube video, 5:36, https://www.desiringgod.org/interviews/what-made-it-okay-for-god-to-kill-women-and-children-in-the-old-testament.

7 Ibid.

8 William Lane Craig, "#16 Slaughter of the Canaanites," Reasonable Faith, August 6, 2007, https://www.reasonablefaith.org/writings/question-answer/slaughter-of-the-canaanites/.

9 Frederick Douglass, *Narrative of the Life of Frederick Douglass: An American Slave* (New York: Cosimo Classics, 2008), 71.

10 This figure was according to the 2001 *World Christian Encyclopedia*, as reported in "Denominations," *Christianity Today*, accessed December 8, 2020, https://www.christianitytoday.com/ct/topics/d/denominations/.

CHAPTER 6

1 Many early church fathers in the fourth and fifth centuries saw a literal reading of the Bible as being the most infantile way of reading. They believed that some Scriptures should not be read literally. This was especially the case when any verses disparaged the good character of God.

2 Peter Enns, *How the Bible Actually Works: In Which I Explain How an Ancient, Ambiguous, and Diverse Book Leads Us to Wisdom Rather Than Answers —and Why That's Great News* (New York: Harper One, 2019), 11.

3 Emphasis added. Italicized Scripture text throughout the book reflects my added emphasis.

4 Throughout the Scriptures we read about the Holy Spirit guiding God's people. As Jesus said, "But when he, the Spirit of truth, comes, he will guide you into all the truth" (John 16:13).

5 An example where you can find one easy all-access location is Bible Study Tools at www.biblestudytools.com.

6 The art of sacred argument involves the ability to have civil disagreements. As Rabbi Ilyse Kramer states in *Tales of the Talmud*, "Sacred Arguing works as a category, when the differing parties agree, not only to disagree; but also, to remain in relationship with one another."

7 The word *haverim* comes from the Hebrew word *haver*, which means friend.

8 Ann Spangler and Lois Tverberg, *Sitting at the Feet of the Rabbi Jesus: How the Jewishness of Jesus Can Transform Your Faith* (Grand Rapids, MI: Zondervan, 2009), 74.

9 See Michael Chernick, "The Lost Art of Argument for the Sake of Heaven," *Michael Chernick* (blog), *Times of Israel*, November 17, 2016, https://blogs .timesofisrael.com/the-lost-art-of-argument-for-the-sake-of-heaven/.

10 Rob Bell, *What Is the Bible? How an Ancient Library of Poems, Letters, and Stories Can Transform the Way You Think and Feel about Everything* (New York: Harper Collins, 2017), 153.

CHAPTER 7

1 To see pictures of this totem, search online for "Air Force Academy Colorado Springs."

2 Phil Zuckerman, "Why Evangelicals Hate Jesus," *Huffington Post*, updated May 25, 2011, https://www.huffpost.com/entry/why-evangelicals-hate-jes_ b_830237.

3 Bill Maher, "New Rules," *HBO Real Time with Bill Maher*, quoted in Brad Jersak, *A More Christlike God* (Pasadena, CA: Plain Truth Ministries, 2015).

4 Gregory A. Boyd, *Crucifixion of the Warrior God*, vol. 1 (Minneapolis: Fortress Press, 2017), xxviii.

5 Gregory A. Boyd, *Crucifixion of the Warrior God*, vol. 2 (Minneapolis: Fortress Press, 2017), 629–30.

6 Brian Zahnd, *Sinners in the Hands of a Loving God: The Scandalous Truth of the Very Good News* (Colorado Springs: Waterbrook, 2017), 26.

7 The KJV states, "all bare him witness." The Young's Literal Translation has it as "all were bearing testimony to him." J. B. Phillips states, "Everybody noticed what he said."

CHAPTER 8

1 Michael McAfee and Lauren Green McAfee, *Not What You Think: Why the Bible Might Be Nothing We Expected Yet Everything We Need* (Grand Rapids, MI: Zondervan, 2019), quoted in John Stonestreet, "Millennials and the Bible: 'Not What You Think,'" *Christian News Journal*, August 20, 2019, https:// christiannewsjournal.com/millennials-and-the-bible-not-what-you-think/.

2 Dmitri Royster, *The Epistle to the Hebrews: A Commentary* (New York: St Vladimir's Seminary Press, 2003), 18.

3 Also see Revelation 19:13, where Jesus is named the Word of God.

CHAPTER 9

1 Taken from Gregory A. Boyd, *Crucifixion of the Warrior God*, vol. 2 (Minneapolis: Fortress Press, 2017), 702.

2 "All Scripture is God-breathed and is useful for teaching, rebuking, correcting and training in righteousness, so that the servant of God may be thoroughly equipped for every good work" (2 Timothy 3:16-17).

3 The name Israel actually means "struggles with God" (see Genesis 32:28).

4 Mirrors in Paul's day were made of polished metal, which reflected a dim, incomplete image of the person who looked into it.

5 It is interesting to note that God accommodated slavery because of Israel's hard hearts after he freed them from slavery in Egypt. This counter-narrative that is so central to the Old Testament clearly reveals that God is a God of freedom and dignity for all peoples and is opposed to slavery.

6 See Psalm 40:6; 51:16; Hosea 6:6; Jeremiah 7:22; Hebrews 10:5-6.

CHAPTER 10

1 Neil Wooten, "Making God in Your Own Image," *Huffington Post*, January 23, 2014.

2 Taken from a true story I heard on Greg Boyd's podcast, *ReKnew*. I have made some minor changes to this story to help build on it as a great metaphor of God's loving accommodation on our behalf.

3 Matthew J. Korpman, *Saying No to God: A Radical Approach to Reading the Bible Faithfully* (Orange, CA: Quoir, 2019), chapter 10.

4 Gregory A. Boyd, *Cross Vision: How the Crucifixion of Jesus Makes Sense of Old Testament Violence* (Minneapolis: Fortress Press, 2017), 52.

5 Ibid., 52–53.

6 Gregory A. Boyd, *Crucifixion of the Warrior God*, vol. 1 (Minneapolis: Fortress Press, 2017), xxxiv.

7 Ibid., xxxv.

8 Ibid., xxxv.

9 Derek Flood, *Disarming Scripture: Cherry-Picking Liberals, Violence-Loving Conservatives, and Why We All Need to Learn to Read the Bible like Jesus Did* (San Francisco: Metanoia Books, 2014), 27.

10 Paul Copan and Matthew Flannagan, *Did God Really Command Genocide? Coming to Terms with the Justice of God* (Grand Rapids, MI: Baker Books, 2014), 27.

11 Paul's wishes are also tied in to the unique context that Timothy finds himself in regarding a certain church and should not be assumed to be relevant for all churches at all times.

12 A very strong argument can be made that Paul is addressing a specific church struggling with domineering women and that his opinion is a personal desire for this unique situation and not the norm for all churches at all times. Basically, a point can be made that any form of domination, by any group of people, regardless of their gender, must be silenced.

13 I wouldn't want to argue with Jesus concerning the words he spoke. The patriarchs are the source of these laws, but Moses enforced them upon Israel. In this way Moses did what Jesus said, as he "gave you circumcision."

PART THREE EPIGRAPH

Keith Giles, *Jesus Unbound: Liberating the Word of God from the Bible* (Orange, CA: Quoir, 2018), 26.

CHAPTER 11

1 Gregory A. Boyd, *Crucifixion of the Warrior God*, vol. 2 (Minneapolis: Fortress Press, 2017), 810.

2 Stephen S. Pearce, "Judge a Society by Its Hospitality," Reform Judaism, accessed December 10, 2020, https://reformjudaism.org/learning/torah -study/vayeira/judge-society-its-hospitality.

3 We read in 2 Peter 2:5 that Noah was a "preacher of righteousness."

4 One interesting thought to keep in mind when we come across water as a vessel of violence is that ancient Middle Eastern religion believed that evil gods controlled the waters that they thought surrounded the earth. In this way God could be seen as holding these evil powers at bay. In the flood story, God re-leases his hands of protection, resulting in these evil spirits destroying the earth. This is also seen in the story of Israel crossing the Red Sea. God held back the evil powers to let Israel pass through the waters, but when the Egyptian armies entered the sea they were drowned because they did not have God's protection over evil. We also see the potential presence of evil spirits behind Jesus rebuk-ing the wind and waves when he calmed the storm in Mark 4:35-41.

5 Speaking of the exodus, it is also interesting to note that it was a "destroyer" that killed the firstborn males in Egypt (Exodus 12:23). The text does not state it was God. This destroyer very easily could have been a demonic power that was allowed to kill when God released his hands of protection over Egypt because of the hardness of their hearts because of sin.

CHAPTER 12

1 There are other times we see this principle of God honoring the freedom of those to whom he gives power.

2 John Piper, "What Made It Okay for God to Kill Women and Children in the Old Testament?" Desiring God, February 27, 2010, https://www .desiringgod.org/interviews/what-made-it-okay-for-god-to-kill-women-and -children-in-the-old-testament.

3 Bodie Hodge, "Isn't the God of the Old Testament Harsh, Brutal, and Downright Evil?," Answers in Genesis, March 27, 2015, https:// answersingenesis.org/who-is-god/isnt-the-god-of-the-old-testament-harsh -brutal-and-downright-evil/.

4 Tim Nester, "Genocide and 'Holy War' in the Old Testament," Focus on the Family, accessed December 9, 2020, https://www.focusonthefamily.com/ family-qa/genocide-and-holy-war-in-the-old-testament/.

5 Richard Dawkins, *The God Delusion* (New York: Mariner Books, 2008), 51.

6 One example is Peter Enns, *The Bible Tells Me So: Why Defending Scripture Has Made Us Unable to Read It* (Grand Rapids, MI: HarperOne, 2014). There is some debate regarding the archaeological arguments for or against the conquest narratives, so none of this is settled.

7 Paul Copan and Matthew Flannagan, *Did God Really Command Genocide? Com-ing to Terms with the Justice of God* (Grand Rapids, MI: Baker Books, 2014), 99.

8 Also see Exodus 33:2; 34:24; Numbers 32:21; Deuteronomy 4:27, 38; 7:1, 20, 22-23.

9 Preston Sprinkle, *Fight: A Christian Case for Non-Violence* (David C Cook, 2013), chap. 4, para. 20, Kindle.

CHAPTER 13

1 Quoted in "Book Excerpt: Hitchens's 'God Is Not Great,'" *Newsweek*, August 21, 2007, https://www.newsweek.com/book-excerpt-hitchenss-god -not-great-99357.

2 I have heard it said that "fear not" is mentioned 365 times in the Bible. One "fear not" for each day of the year.

3 John MacArthur, *Revelation 12–22* (Chicago: Moody, 2000), 117–18.

4 Quoted in *Relevant*, August 28, 2007.

5 Ronald J. Sider, *If Jesus Is Lord: Loving Our Enemies in an Age of Violence* (Grand Rapids, MI: Baker Academic, 2019), 96.

6 Ibid., 97.

7 Steve Gregg, *Revelation: Four Views*, rev. ed. (Nashville: Thomas Nelson, 2013), 506. Quoting David S. Clark.

8 Jesus' teaching on the end times is known as the Olivet Discourse, as he spoke these words on the Mount of Olives and in the temple near the Mount of Olives. They are found in Matthew 24–25; Mark 13; Luke 21.

9 Peter Schafer, *The History of the Jews in Antiquity: The Jews of Palestine from Alexander the Great to the Arab Conquest* (New York: Routledge, 1995), 191–92.

10 Dispensationalism is a theological view and method of biblical interpretation that views God interacting with humanity in different ways through seven unique ages known as dispensations.

11 John H. Walton and Craig S. Keener, ed., *NIV Cultural Backgrounds Study Bible* (Grand Rapids, MI: Zondervan, 2016), 2097.

12 Robert Jamieson, A. R. Fausset, and David Brown, *Commentary Critical and Explanatory on the Whole Bible* (1871). This work is in the public domain and is available at http://www.jesuseveryday.com/free_christian_books/ Jamieson_Fausset_Brown-Commentary_on_the_Whole_Bible.pdf.

CHAPTER 14

1 John Piper, "Putting My Daughter to Bed Two Hours after the Bridge Collapsed," Desiring God, August 1, 2007, https://www.desiringgod.org/ articles/putting-my-daughter-to-bed-two-hours-after-the-bridge-collapsed.

2 Clark Pinnock et al., *The Openness of God: A Biblical Challenge to the Traditional Understanding of God* (Downers Grove, IL: InterVarsity Press, 1994), 7.

3 See Greg Boyd, "Analogies for Understanding Prayer," Renew, July 30, 2014, https://reknew.org/2014/07/analogies-for-understanding-prayer/.

4 Watchman Nee, *The Prayer Ministry of the Church* (New York: Christian Fellowship, 1973), 23.

CHAPTER 15

1 John Wesley Hanson, *Universalism, the Prevailing Doctrine of the Christian Church during Its First Five Hundred Years* (Pantianos Classics, 1899), 95.

2 John Wesley Hanson researched church history and quotes other scholars claiming that patristic universalism was the most dominant view of the early church. See ibid.

3 Steve Gregg, *All You Want to Know about Hell: Three Christian Views of God's Final Solution to the Problem of Sin* (Nashville, Thomas Nelson, 2013), 8.

4 Ibid., 72.

5 Bradley Jersak, *Her Gates Will Never Be Shut: Hope, Hell, and the New Jerusalem* (Eugene, OR: Wipf and Stock, 2009), 39.

6 David Bentley Hart, *The New Testament: A Translation* (New Haven, CT: Yale University Press, 2017), 538.

7 Ibid., 53.

8 See Bradley Jersak, "Hell Is a Kingdom," *Clarion: Journal for Religion, Peace, and Justice*, December 18, 2015, 3, https://www.clarion-journal.com/files/hell-is-a-kingdom.pdf.

9 Ibid., 6.

10 Ibid., 6.

CHAPTER 16

1 John Piper, panel discussion at the Desiring God 2008 National Conference, transcript available at https://www.desiringgod.org/interviews/panel-discussion-piper-driscoll-and-ferguson.

2 "In Christ Alone" track 1 on Keith Getty and Stuart Townend, *Lord of Every Heart*, Thankyou Music, 2001.

3 The view that God had to be appeased through the substitutionary death of Jesus was not even a consideration during the first thousand years of the early church.

4 *Christus Victor* means Christ the Victor.

5 All throughout the Gospels we read about the centrality of Jesus' ministry of bringing the kingdom of God to earth.

6 Bradley Jersak, *A More Christlike God: A More Beautiful Gospel* (Pasadena, CA: Plain Truth Ministries, 2015), 234.

7 Brian Zahnd, *Sinners in the Hands of a Loving God: The Scandalous Truth of the Very Good News* (New York: Waterbrook, 2017), 82.

A FINAL WORD

1 Kieran Kavanaugh, ed., *John of the Cross: Selected Writings* (New York: Paulist Press, 1987), 67.

The Author

COLIN McCARTNEY has worked in urban missions for over thirty-five years. He is the founder of two urban ministries and the author of *The Beautiful Disappointment, Red Letter Revolution*, and along with his wife, Judith, *What Does Justice Look Like and Why Does God Care about It?* He has appeared on Canadian television and radio and published articles in national newspapers regarding urban issues. He is a mentor to pastors and businesspeople and serves as a ministry trainer and coach. He is also a popular speaker and currently leads an urban church-planting movement called Connect City.